Educating Children with Emotional and Behavioural Difficulties

This book offers practical guidance on teaching children with emotional and behavioural difficulties in the mainstream school. The authors acknowledge the challenges involved in teaching children with behavioural difficulties, but argue that it is possible to include them in mainstream education to the benefit of all involved.

Educating Children with Emotional and Behavioural Difficulties provides an accessible and ground-breaking approach to dealing with the inclusive classroom. The book focuses on developing teachers' individual skills, attitudes and classroom practices within a whole school approach to help the ordinary school provide for such children. The approach evolved from a detailed study of a school recognised by Ofsted as successfully integrating children with emotional and behavioural difficulties, and the book includes detailed case studies to illustrate the principles in action.

All teachers committed to inclusive education will find this book essential reading.

John Thacker is Senior Lecturer in Education at Exeter University.

Dave Strudwick has worked as a SENCo and an advisory teacher with Devon's Behaviour Support Team.

Elly Babbedge is a full-time Primary School Teacher.

School Concerns series

Edited by Peter Blatchford
Institute of Education, University of London

This topical new series addresses key issues that are causing concern in schools. Each book is based around a case study school which is used to illustrate and contextualise best practice whilst showing the real implications of current research on the everyday classroom.

The books provide an innovative and accessible approach to dealing with the inclusive classroom and are written by leading names in their respective fields. They will be essential reading for teachers, heads of department, headteachers and policy-makers determined to address the key concerns in education today.

Supporting Inclusive Education
Jenny Corbett

Educating Children with Emotional and Behavioural Difficulties
John Thacker, Dave Strudwick and Elly Babbedge

Bullying
Sonia Sharp, Tiny Arora and David Thompson

Enhancing PSHE
Sally Inman, Martin Buck and Miles Tandy

Underachievement in Schools
Anne West

Educating Children with Emotional and Behavioural Difficulties

Inclusive practice in mainstream schools

John Thacker, Dave Strudwick and Elly Babbedge

LONDON AND NEW YORK

First published 2002
by RoutledgeFalmer
11 New Fetter Lane, London EC4P 4EE

Simultaneously published in the USA and Canada
by RoutledgeFalmer
29 West 35th Street, New York, NY 10001

Reprinted 2003

RoutledgeFalmer is an imprint of the Taylor & Francis Group

Typeset in Sabon by BC Typesetting, Bristol
Printed and bound in Great Britain by
Biddles Ltd, Guildford and King's Lynn

British Library Cataloguing in Publication Data
A catalogue record for this book is available from the British Library

Library of Congress Cataloging in Publication Data
Thacker, V. J. (Vincent John)
Educating children with emotional and behavioural difficulties:
inclusive practice in mainstream schools/Vincent John Thacker,
Dave Strudwick, and Elly Babbedge.
p. cm.–(School concerns series)
Includes bibliographical references and index.
ISBN 0–415–23050–0 – ISBN 0–415–23051–9 (pbk.)
1. Problem children–Education–Great Britain. 2. Behaviour
modification. 3. Mainstreaming in education–Great Britain.
I. Struckwick, Dave, 1966– 11. Babbedge, Elly, 1952– 111.Title. IV Series.

LC4803.G7 T43 2001
371.93–dc21

2001049063

ISBN 0–415–23050–0 (hbk)
ISBN 0–415–23051–9 (pbk)

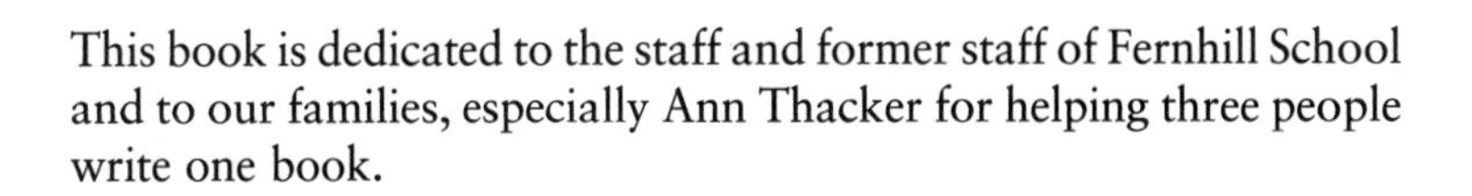

This book is dedicated to the staff and former staff of Fernhill School and to our families, especially Ann Thacker for helping three people write one book.

Contents

Preface: Series Introduction

School staff face many challenges today. Recently they have had to respond to a plethora of curriculum and assessment reforms, Literacy and Numeracy Strategies, Government-led moves toward performance indicators, regular Ofsted inspections, and a general push toward accountability and raising achievement levels of pupils. But there are other, possibly more enduring, concerns that also affect the day-to-day functioning of schools.

I get insight into these concerns in the course of one of my professional responsibilities – supervising teachers who are undertaking research for dissertations, as part of MA level courses. When choosing a topic I encourage them to reflect on their own professional concerns and ways in which they can shed light on them. The range of topics are rich and varied and in recent years have included underachievement of particular groups in school, student motivation and attitudes, bullying, effective approaches to inclusion in classrooms, and pupils' emotional and social difficulties. Some issues are made particularly pressing because of recent events in their own or neighbouring schools, and are high on agendas of current educational and political discussion, as well as at staff meetings.

However, too often the information teachers and others need on these topics is not available in a form that they find helpful or accessible. Sometimes the topic is addressed in a way that is too academic and removed from the practical concerns of everyday school life. But there is a converse problem that seems to have become more obvious recently – a tendency to oversimplify and trivialise what is likely to be a complex issue, and offer packaged solutions instead of a full analysis.

This book series – School Concerns – has been set up to bridge the gap between these two types of approach. It was designed to address contemporary issues, usually related to behaviour in schools, that are cause for concern. The aim of each book in the Series is to summarise and evaluate relevant research evidence and theory, and to seek to provide insights, conclusions and suggestions of value to readers, and to relate research findings and theory to classroom concerns. The Series is designed to be helpful but to avoid a 'cookbook' approach, to do justice to the complexity of a topic while avoiding dense argument and jargon. This is a difficult balance to achieve, but each author has been chosen because it was felt that not only were they leading authorities on particular topics, but they would also be able to make the topics accessible to a wide audience.

The publishers were keen to start the Series because, as far as they knew, there has not been an attempt to cover these kinds of issues in a unified and accessible fashion. The Series covers both primary and secondary sectors.

Each author has been asked to think carefully about the potential readers of the book. We have asked each author to include, as an integral part of their book, a case study of a class or school and to use this to illustrate and exemplify key ideas and conclusions. The books should be of interest to all in schools, to tutors and students on Initial Teacher Training and Professional Development Courses, as well as to researchers and lecturers, LEA and Government staff. The books will also be of interest to a wider and more general audience, for example parents. Some issues are of obvious international interest and authors have been encouraged, where appropriate, to draw out conclusions of relevance overseas.

This is a timely and exciting Series, and I expect the books to provide a significant contribution to educational debate.

Introduction to this book

This is a rewarding and fascinating book. It offers an analysis, and an approach, to the education of children with emotional and behavioural difficulties in mainstream schools, which are insightful and helpful. The authors are remarkably successful, I feel, in bringing together the perspectives of researcher, class teacher and special educational needs coordinator to provide a thorough coverage of the field, which is firmly grounded in the everyday experience of children and teachers. It manages to offer realistic solutions and points for reflection without over simplifying. I am sure that all interested readers will find the book empowering and informative. It covers amongst other things the role of group work, a systemic approach, and home school relations.

It is also a challenging book. It does not avoid the real difficulties some children present. At its heart is the timely reminder that education is about relationships and social and emotional factors as much as academic progress. The authors manage to show how the challenges posed by some children can benefit teachers and other children; in the words of a headteacher, to the surprised parents of a child with severe difficulties: 'He will be a gift to the school.' The messages in this book deserve a wide readership.

Professor Peter Blatchford
Institute of Education, University of London

List of abbreviations

AWCEBD	Association of Workers for Children with Emotional and Behavioural Difficulties
DES	Department of Education and Science (now DfEE Department for Education and Employment)
EBD	Emotional and Behavioural Difficulties
ESN	Educationally Subnormal
IEP	Individual Education Plan
Inset	In-service training
ICT	Information Communications Technology
IT	Information Technology
LSA	Learning Support Assistant
MTA	Meal-time Assistant
Ofsted	Office for Standards in Education
PE	Physical Education
SATs	Standard Assessment Tasks
SEN	Special Educational Needs
SENCo	Special Educational Needs Coordinator

Introduction

This book consists of an approach to teaching, suitable for all children, which we apply to the education of children with EBD in the ordinary school.[1] The book is timely since, at the heart of our philosophy, is a commitment to inclusion. This emphasis on maintaining pupils with special educational needs in mainstream schools has been present in official documents from the Warnock Report (DES, 1978) and the 1981 Education Act to the 1997 Green Paper 'Excellence for All Children: Meeting Special Educational Needs'. This has been based partly on a wish to avoid stigmatising children and partly because evidence does not show significant educational gains for children attending special schools (see, for example, Roe, 1965).

While recent educational reforms such as the publication of 'league tables' seem opposed to this trend of inclusion by encouraging the early removal of pupils who are seen as too demanding of time and limited resources, we believe that it is possible to keep children with emotional and behavioural difficulties in ordinary schools with profit to them and to the other children in the school. We have researched and taught in a school, which we called 'Fernhill', which made a practice of responding to parental requests to accept children who had been excluded from neighbouring schools because of their difficult behaviour. This school received an Ofsted inspection which noted that the school had successfully integrated these pupils and noted that otherwise these children might have

1 For reasons of space and economy we will make use of abbreviations and contractions such as children with EBD for children with emotional and behavioural difficulties. These are contained in a list of abbreviations on p. xii.

gone into residential special schooling. The Ofsted report went on to say that the quality of provision for these children was seen as very good and that they were receiving a broad and balanced curriculum in the company of their peers (see Thacker, 1998, p. 406).

Working with the whole school staff of eighteen or so teachers, the first author of the present book developed a cooperative approach to research, in which all the staff were involved including the second and third authors. We looked at leadership and organisational culture (which might be briefly defined as 'the way we do things around here') by examining the everyday practice of the head and staff over a period of one year. During this time we developed a 'grounded theory' of the way the head exercised leadership and the way that he and the staff interacted and created the organisational culture. These findings inform our whole-school approach set out in chapter 4.

In the second year of research we looked at how the culture helped the teachers deal with difficult children. We also looked at how this culture influenced, and was influenced by, good classroom practice and, as part of this two-year study, the first author, John, observed the third author, Elly, teaching over a school term. He then wrote up the findings of the complete study in the form of a published book (Thacker, 1998) while the third author, Elly, continued to develop her approach, remaining at the school as a classteacher. The second author, Dave, who had been special educational needs coordinator (SENCo) at the school, extended his experience by becoming an advisory teacher working with a behaviour support team responsible for working with teachers in many primary schools in support of children with emotional and behavioural difficulties.

In the present book, we continue the research process by examining many case studies of children with EBD carried out by Elly and Dave working with children with EBD over a period of about four years. What we discovered about good teaching principles provides the summary at the end of chapter 3 of this book.

Thus the approach we put forward in this book has been well tested in practice by two of the authors and closely scrutinised in a research process by the remaining author. We have also drawn widely on the work of other teachers with children with EBD both at primary and secondary phases of education and in chapter 1 we put our approach into a historical context of approaches to the treatment and education of these children. Our purpose for the rest of the chapter and book is systematically to set out our educational principles so that you will find points to reflect upon, giving you the opportunity to draw out school and classroom implications from the text. It is not a 'tips for teachers' book but it will set you thinking about your own school and classroom and how you can make a difference. One of our major themes in this book is the idea that, while we look at a wide range of systemic factors to help our understanding of children with EBD, other professionals may need to deal with some of these, while our role as teachers may properly constrain us to take action largely within the school. An example in practice would be that while a child's emotional adjustment and educational progress might be affected by conditions of poverty and poor housing, there is little a teacher can do to change these factors directly. However, rather than being pessimistic about progress as shown by the statement 'Oh what can you expect from a background like that!' we would do better to look at what we can change in school which may have a bearing. It might be only something as small as the provision of a homework room, but this may help an individual child overcome some problems arising from overcrowded housing. It is primarily within-school factors which we will concentrate on in the book.

As the book proceeds we aim to build your knowledge of what you might do to become a more resilient and effective teacher. We do this by first looking at personal attitudes and skills, then by taking a detailed look at class management skills before considering how the resources of the whole school might be mobilised to help. We then look at how your influence might be extended by working closely with parents, and the book ends with a chapter where we look at the fine-tuning of a plan to help an individual when all the other aspects of good practice have been considered. Having provided you with these principles and examples of the work in action, we leave you with the ownership of the problem and the scope for creative thinking: the freedom to really make a difference.

The structure of most of the chapters is similar in that we usually start by describing principles based on our work and that of other workers and then illustrate the principles in operation via carefully chosen case studies. Through case studies we explore not only the children's experiences and the perceptions of the peer group but we also follow the personal struggles, reflections and success of adults working with the children. These case studies demonstrate those hard-to-describe subtle details of implementation necessary for teachers to be able to see the fine details of applying this approach.

At the end of chapter 1 we show that how we, as teachers, view emotional disturbance has a great deal to do with how we approach the subject. We state that our starting point is that whatever we do to help children with EBD to cope with school will also be of benefit to the rest of the children. Indeed we believe that children with EBD might be seen as bringing benefits to the rest of the class by making a school confront issues and change to become a more humane place for all. In this way an inclusive school is one where all are welcome and provided for.

Chapter 2 looks at how the teacher can become more resilient and effective by examining his or her attitudes towards these children.

In chapter 3 we look at ideas, especially group-work skills for teachers to consider and use to develop their classroom practice.

Chapter 4 looks at what more is possible for children with EBD when the resources of the school are brought to bear and how a classteacher can contribute to this process.

Chapter 5 looks at the home–school relationships and how teachers can provide expert support on teaching and learning so that parents can share the education of their child.

Finally, chapter 6 brings together all these approaches and shows how the fine-tuning is done when making a plan for an individual child.

Let us finish this introduction by listening to the voices of some teachers who have seen things in a different way and those of some of the children we will be meeting in the case studies.

Teachers

'I had no idea how well the children in this class knew Sam. When I worked with them I found out about all sorts of strategies they used to support him in class and at playtimes that I hadn't noticed.'

'I thought I was a teacher who listened to children but I suddenly realised that I'd missed some of the most obvious things.'

'What a relief to realise that it wasn't a question of dreaming up newer and better things to do: it was about changing my viewpoint, subtle changes, really, but self-supporting and able to grow . . .'

Children

What do people think of you?

'We're bad.'
'They only see us when we're hitting people not when we're good.'
'Appalled by our behaviour.'

How would you like to be seen?

'I'd like people to know what I'm really like and see that good side of me.'
'To be seen as clever, instead of mucking about.'
'I'd like to be seen as caring, kind and gentle.'
'Hope people can see the person inside.'
'Not to have to be tough, to be able to show my feelings.'
'I'd like to be doing good things and not bad things.'

We all recognise children who might state thoughts like these. We intend this book to provide a suitable approach to working with such children.

Chapter 1

Educational approaches to children with EBD

History of educational approaches

In this chapter we will look at the ways in which emotionally and behaviourally disturbed children have been seen over the past century and this includes the changing social factors and educational 'fashions'. Presently dominant positions, including our own, show a stress on the importance of the context, where the child is seen as embedded in networks of relationships which create meaning, and where understanding is aided by considering all the elements in these networks. This view is the systemic (often called ecosystemic) perspective in the literature. In this approach, problem behaviour is seen as an emergent property of a situation that includes the child and the family in the community as well as the behaviour of the teachers and the influences of the school environment. It is no longer seen, simplistically, as behaviour for which the child is totally responsible or which results from a condition which the child 'has', like some illness. There has been a broad swing from a medical approach towards a more educationally based approach. However, it should not be forgotten that to conceptualise the child as needing medical help implied a non-punitive therapeutic approach which was, in its day, a real advance over former views of the child. In these the child was seen as being 'wicked' or as having 'bad blood' or possessed by some demon and in need of strict correction, punishment or even exorcism.

Along with the medical view, which developed in the early years of the twentieth century, the focus of 'treatment' moved out of the mainstream educational context and the early methods were deployed in residential provision. The terminology of the time was of 'maladjustment' as a category of handicap. This was defined in the 1945 regulations (Ministry of Education, 1945) as children showing 'evidence of emotional instability or psychological disturbance' which required 'special educational treatment in order to effect their personal, social or educational readjustment'. In keeping with this medical emphasis, the provision was made through doctors and on to psychiatrists working in child guidance clinics. This whole system has been likened to an 'out-patients' department of the medical model with the special schools acting something like an observation ward! Again, without stretching the comparison too far, the role of educational psychologists in testing, the role of psychiatric social workers in counselling families and the role of teachers in providing reports on behaviour all fitted in neatly with the concept of the medical team. Children would be 'ascertained' as maladjusted by the psychiatrist, their progress would be regularly assessed at case conferences presided over by the psychiatrist, and, if sufficient progress had been made, the decision to 'deascertain' and readmit to the mainstream of education would be made by the psychiatrist. There is no wonder that the whole process was seen as one of outside experts taking the child out of the normal educational provision which, by implication, made it appear that the ordinary classroom teacher did not have the resources to deal with the problem.

In 1955 there were only thirty-six state schools for maladjusted pupils and these were much influenced by the freedom of expression models in education and drew on psychotherapeutic ideas, only looking to classroom experience as source material (see, for example, Lennhoff, 1960; Shaw, 1965; Burn, 1964). Problem behaviour was seen resulting from failures of early experience and so the emphasis was on building relationships before building educational skills.

This may be seen in the following quote from David Wills: 'There are many pathological conditions which, given a warm, restful, non-provocative environment can be self-healing. Many forms of maladjustment are of that kind, and the children will heal themselves if only people will stop "doing things" to them' (Wills, 1960, p. 19).

This led to the idea of 'milieu therapy' where residential schools were run like a family where there are predictable expectations and consistent discipline together with an acceptance that the behaviour of its members is not always going to be perfect.

Such schools offered respite, relationships and what was known as resignification – a rebuilding of self-esteem. Especially in the writing and practice of David Wills, the notion of self-governance was important. The school made many decisions on the basis of community meetings that involved the young people in the process of group rule-making and enforcement.

With the rise in influence of educational psychologists in the 1960s and 70s, the influence of educationalists was brought back into the process. Government advice such as Circular 2/75 (DES, 1975) now saw decisions about 'maladjusted pupils' as educational decisions and not medical.

Underlying models

Over this same time, we see a change from psychodynamic explanations linked to psychiatry, to behavioural models linked to psychologists. A key feature of psychodynamic approaches is that of the unconscious, or an inner psychic world, not normally accessible to conscious thought but exerting a powerful influence upon our feelings and behaviour. Thus to concentrate on removing or suppressing the symptom without tackling the underlying problem is seen to be of limited value. The aims of treatment-based education was to understand the cause of the internal pressures and, in many schools, there was development of a 'cathartic' ethos encouraging the acting-out of instinctual impulses.

It is important to realise that when we talk about a model becoming dominant this does not mean that the previous model is altogether abandoned. There may be attacks and counter-attacks in the literature but this is more about the adherents of one model defining their territory or 'turf'. This is best seen as a professional power struggle as much as any seeking after truth. In the fullness of time, when the dust has died down, we are able to see the virtues of at least some aspects of the former approaches. There are many aspects of the work of pioneers such as Wills that is now widely admired, particularly his stress on self-governance, but the stress on residential work would probably be seen in a less favourable light.

Historically the increasing influence of psychologists who brought the 'treatment' of children with EBD back into the mainstream educational field was associated with the rise of behaviour modification. This is based upon psychological learning principles and makes no assumptions about the unconscious, but concentrates on dealing with the 'symptoms' directly through manipulation of the environment, especially the consequences that follow behaviour. It is a here-and-now approach which looks at the antecedents, behaviour and consequences of actions and tries to change the arrangements, particularly of the consequences, to support a change of behaviour in a desired direction using learning principles.

There was considerable success reported in the use of behavioural methods with this group, which helped raise the profile of behavioural approaches (e.g. Burland, 1978). The approach also contains a move away from simple ascriptions of problems to individual psychopathology towards seeing them as a part of a complex interactive process (e.g. D'Zurilla and Goldfried, 1971).

However a more general feature was equally important and this was the focus on the classroom not the clinic. Teachers were seen as being able to learn the psychological principles and apply them to children with EBD in their own classrooms. Often such work was introduced and encouraged by educational psychologists who were widely involved in the training of teachers in these behavioural methods.

A third model, and one that was introduced alongside the other two, was drawn from humanistic psychology, where the individual is seen as unique. Thus, he or she pays attention to his/her perception of him/herself and others rather than to any reductionist objective descriptions. The prime quality required is empathy, to put oneself in another's place. The main techniques deployed would be working in small groups, learning to listen carefully and to understand others' points of view while being heard oneself. The result is a general gain in self-image which counteracts the destructive nature of the pathological peer group, which is only concerned with conformity and control. This approach was associated with psychologists using ideas from Carl Rogers and George Kelly (e.g. Rogers, 1983; Kelly, 1955).

As we saw above, a general effect of the move to a more educational/psychological approach rather than a medical/psychiatric one involved a change from seeing children as treated by distant experts to a consultative model, initially behaviourally based, which saw teachers as being skilled enough and well placed to help. Although psychodynamic, behavioural and humanistic viewpoints continue to be influential, there has been a shift towards systemic viewpoints, especially ecosystemic, where the child is seen as embedded in networks of relationships which create meaning, and where understanding is aided by considering all the elements in these networks. In the next section we will look at the various influences on children which, in some cases, are expressed as emotional and behavioural disturbance.

Definitions of EBD

Almost all past terminology has suggested that the child 'has' the condition and is somehow at fault. The definition of EBD in the Government Circular 23/89 (DES, 1989) writes of 'children who set up barriers between themselves and their learning environment through inappropriate, aggressive, bizarre or withdrawn behaviour' and who 'have developed a range of strategies for dealing with day-to-day experiences which are inappropriate and impede normal personal and social development, and make it difficult for them to learn'.

This ignores the social context, and Ravenette (1972) questioned whether the earlier maladjusted label was for the benefit of the child or the needs of the school. Galloway and Goodwin (1987) drew a distinction between a child 'disturbed' in him/herself and/or who was 'disturbing' to others to signal this same idea. Such ideas have cut little official or classroom ice. It may be that they act, as Szasz (1972) called them, as 'mental tranquillisers' which take away the need for organisations to look at themselves. Anyone who refuses to conform to what is laid down can be explained away as disturbed, thus taking away the need for the school to look at how it functions. The term maladjusted, while implying that a solution could be changing either or both the child and the environment, very often implied in practice that the problem resides in the child and it is he or she who must be treated and cured.

One reason for this is that children with EBD, while failing to learn successfully, like other children with SEN, often also interfere with the learning of other pupils and challenge the personal authority and competence of teachers by non-cooperative and oppositional behaviours. The fact that children with EBD are disturbing to teachers is the unifying feature. As Cooper (1999b, pp. 9–10) says:

> Beyond this there is little evidence to suggest that the different emotional and behavioural manifestations that are given the EBDs label are related to a single condition. Students' emotional difficulties may manifest themselves in terms of extreme withdrawal from social involvement leading to social isolation

> within school or school refusal. At another level, the student with emotional difficulties may simply be preoccupied with emotional concerns to the extent that this interferes with the learning process [and] may be involved in bullying either as victims or perpetrators. The most commonly cited forms of behavioural disturbance in classrooms take the form of unauthorised student talk, the hindrance of other pupils from working as well as forms of student behaviour that directly challenge the authority of the teacher. Rarer, but more severe, manifestations include hyperactivity, bullying, problem sexual behaviour and damage to property.

Johnston *et al.* (1992) found that attributions regarding the origin of (or blame for) the behaviour depended on the type of behaviour. Adults held children less responsible for hyperactive behaviour and were likely to excuse such behaviour, whereas aggressive behaviour was considered to be more within the child's control and attracted more negative reactions.

What is the role of teachers?

A broad movement involves people like Rutter (e.g. Rutter, 1976) and similar epidemiologists who try to establish correlations between emotional 'health' and socio-economic factors like housing, birth factors, etc. Their aim is to alert us to the multiplicity of factors in any situation and help formulate general social policy. Since the associations are correlational and not causal, they need to be interpreted with caution. This makes them useful enough to justify policy moves, like improving the housing stock, but they are not much use, in a day-to-day sense, to classroom teachers except as part of their general role as citizens or as collaborators in community-wide action. And yet, as we shall see, the behaviour of children is often blamed on their poor home backgrounds by teachers looking for explanations.

This points up one of the central dilemmas for people working in this field. As seen in the work of Rutter mentioned above, there is good correlational evidence linking mental health with socio-economic factors such as poor housing and poverty. However, while these links are correlational and statistically significant, there are always cases of children with poor home backgrounds who do not develop EBD. This suggests that more than one factor is at work and, while we should tackle poverty and poor housing as part of an overall policy, we need to be cautious in attributing this or that factor in any particular case. Yet, when faced with a child showing EBD, teachers tend to blame home factors. In a survey of 428 junior classteachers carried out in 61 schools across 10 Local Education Authorities, Croll and Moses (1985) showed that two-thirds of behaviour or discipline problems were thought, by the teachers, to be due to home factors; a third to within-child factors, and in only two to four out of a hundred cases to any school or teacher factors including previous schools or teachers.

> Indeed the Elton Report (Department of Education and Science, 1989, p. 133) says that: 'Our evidence suggests that teachers' picture of parents is generally very negative. Many teachers feel that parents are to blame for much misbehaviour in schools. We consider that, while this picture contains an element of truth, it is distorted.'

Apart from any questions of distortion, we need to be careful that using such explanations does not distract us from the search to find something we can influence as teachers. Thus, while we may use the role of poor housing and poverty in producing a fertile breeding-ground for poor behaviour when seeking a complete explanation, we still have to work with young people from poor material conditions and in many cases may be better advised to concentrate on our classroom management techniques, for example, as a guide to action on behalf of children with EBD. As we said in the Introduction this is one of our major themes in this book – the idea that, while we may look at a wide range of systemic factors to help our understanding of children with EBD, we may need the help of other professionals to deal with these. Our role may properly constrain us to taking action within the school, and teachers should concentrate on within-school factors. Thus, while there is a limit to the amount we can do about poor housing, we can influence the social relationships in our classrooms.

Schools can make a difference

This is a relatively new area of research. As Cooper *et al.* (1994, p. 19) say, there was, until very recently, a focus on individual and family pathology 'with little attention being given as to how the school may exacerbate, and sometimes actually cause, behaviour problems'. This has been rapidly changing over the last two decades and we shall now look at some of the research which provides strong indications that there are many aspects of school which, as teachers, we can affect and which affect children's social and emotional functioning.

As early as 1967 Power *et al.* (1967) reported large differences between the delinquency rates of a London borough's twenty secondary schools. These differences, they argued, could not be explained in terms of differences in the intake of children but were due to factors in the schools themselves. Although we are taking this as encouraging evidence that schools and teachers can make a difference, the political effect at the time was an uncomfortable one for those schools which 'failed' to protect their children from delinquency and this effect could no longer be deflected entirely on to family influences. Partly for this reason, it was some time before similar studies were carried out, for example that of Rutter *et al.* (1979, p. 52) which pointed to 'within-school' factors which helped to determine delinquency rates and led to their suggestion that 'some schools may be successful in protecting children from the risks of delinquency, although they live in neighbourhoods where many children come before the courts. Conversely, other schools may be exposing children who live in delinquency-free neighbourhoods to such a risk.'

While these studies were concerned with delinquency, Burt and Howard (1974, p. 130) listed a number of school experiences or conditions significantly associated with maladjustment, which as we have seen, is an older term for the current EBD label. These conditions included:

1. uncongenial teachers who were unsympathetic and lacked understanding;
2. uncongenial pupils who teased, bullied or generally made life difficult for their peers;
3. absence from or change of school;
4. placement in a class where the work was too difficult.

Bunt and Howard based these findings on a large number of their case studies spanning twenty years, which showed that transfer to another school was 'followed by a complete and apparently permanent disappearance of every overt sign of maladjustment' (1974, p. 130).

This is very encouraging in showing that there is an important contribution to be made via school factors to which we can make a difference.

Of particular interest to us is the idea of school culture or ethos both at a school as well as at a classroom level. This is in line with modern research approaches, including our own (see Thacker, 1998), together with a swing towards a focus on the classroom and teachers. Chapters 3 and 4 of this book reflect the importance of this trend.

Taking this approach makes us, as teachers, feel more effective and less frustrated because we are focusing on things over which we have control, and are not spending our effort on things we cannot really influence.

This is not to say that we ignore the very real effect home background has on behaviour but we tackle it from the perspective of how classroom teachers, working with parents, can make a difference. This is the substance of chapter 5.

Nature of explanations

Let us turn to the idea that how teachers see the explanation of a child's behaviour will make a difference as to how they act. For example, it can be helpful to some people to draw a distinction between *internal* and *external* influences on children with EBD. *Internal* influences are constitutional factors such as birth damage or a genetic condition. Such explanations are located in the medical model we looked at earlier, and enable people to be tolerant of subsequent difficult behaviour on the lines of 'he can't help it – he's autistic'. If someone is seen as 'sick' this brings with it associated benefits like tolerance and taking pressure off the 'patient'. In our society being sick is usually seen as not your fault (although in some cultures it is seen as evidence of possession by evil forces!). Thus, accepting a particular explanation of EBD behaviour may carry with it a whole set of accompanying assumptions. In this example the explanation may result in some desirable outcomes, in that seeing someone as 'sick' may help people to be more understanding and tolerant.

Unhelpfully, such an explanation for autism, say, or Asperger's syndrome may imply that help needs to be given by an expert and that there is little the person can do to help themselves. We must remember that, at one level, these are labels for a cluster of symptoms such as not sitting still and being withdrawn. A great deal of time may be taken with deciding on the label. This may be appropriate for a psychiatrist or other medical person who then might be able to offer appropriate treatment but a teacher might be better engaged in thinking how to help the 'symptoms' meanwhile (of not sitting still, being withdrawn or whatever) while giving instruction in reading and other academic subjects.

The teacher's best help for the child may be to gain a broad and balanced education. It may be that an important part of such an education is providing the social conditions where an individual with medical problems can share their needs with their peers, ask for help and to seek solutions for ways of coping. We will see examples of this in action in case studies in later chapters.

External influences are such environmental factors as 'poverty' and 'poor housing'. Here the politically right wing may see such things as being due to 'fecklessness' while the left wing might see them as traps which hold people back. Here, a pre-existing political view determines how we interprete a situation.

We do not have to look far for the motivation of teachers who use explanations that locate responsibility for children's behaviour in their home circumstances. As Cooper *et al.* point out:

> This is not surprising given the responsibility of teachers to create effective learning environments for whole classes of pupils and for which there is a need to maintain a certain degree of order and discipline in the classroom. Behaviour problems constitute a direct threat to that responsibility and, at the same time, may be seen as reflecting poorly on the teacher's professional skills and status in the eyes of colleagues, parents and pupils. This tendency towards pupil blame is reinforced by the fact that some instances of behavioural difficulty are initiated by pupils and have their origin in the behaviour of these pupils.
>
> (Cooper *et al.* 1994, p. 15)

Deeper factors

It also raises a deeper set of questions about the nature of explanation. Influencing factors may be differently handled by teachers depending on the theoretical framework adopted by them. For example, psychodynamic thinkers might look for evidence of how well the parent–infant bond was developed: for them attachment theory offers useful approaches to helping. On the other hand, behavioural theorists would not dispute the importance of early experiences, but would look at the behaviour in the here and now as the best guide to intervention. Analysis of such here-and-now behaviour would provide clues as to how the child's environment might be reshaped in order to help the child to relearn more adaptive behaviours. A common factor in both of these frameworks is an assumption that it is possible to know the 'truth' about a situation. This leads to such assumptions that it may be that the client does not see the 'truth' but the psychoanalytic interpreter can see beyond the defence reactions of the client and is thus able to interpret events more accurately than the client. Similarly, workers using behavioural principles see the observation of external behaviour as more 'objective' than the internal view and intention of the client.

However, there has been a growing body of theory that suggests that we can never know objective reality (Gergen, 1985). Instead, people are seen as placing different meanings and interpretations of events according to their view of the world and thus each of us constructs our view of reality. There are a number of extreme versions of this view point but Cooper *et al.* (1994) suggest that 'more balanced views have begun to emerge' and they cite Speed with approval as having a co-contructionist position which accepts that 'a structured reality exists but recognises that reality is constructed or mediated in the sense that different aspects are highlighted according to ideas that individuals or groups have about it' (Speed, 1991, p. 401). This is the point of view that we will also adopt in this book and we thus pay attention to the differing perspectives of all the people involved in a situation which usually involves at least the child, the parents and the teacher.

This point of view helps us to make sense of some situations where a teacher complains of a pupil's irrationality and protest that the child's behaviour is impossible to understand. There is now some empirical evidence that the problem may be one of perspective. Cronk (1987) looked at conflict situations between teachers and pupils and found that outsiders could find evidence that pupils have rational views of what they do despite the teacher's belief that the child is being irrational.

Similarly, different teachers and different schools have different standards and expectations. What will be seen in one school as a major infringement of the rules will not be an issue in another. Attitudes to the wearing of uniforms is an everyday example. This is to be expected, since they reflect the organisational culture of the school, which itself reflects the different values and standards or heart-sets of the staff, as one of the authors refers to them elsewhere (see Thacker, 1994). These attitudes and values determine the degree of acceptance and tolerance of children with EBD which varies across schools. The attitudes and values of the teachers are at the heart of the matter as we shall demonstrate in the next chapter.

More formal ways of looking at the subjective nature of behaviour problems is provided by social theorists like Kitsuse (1962) who have looked at the process of social construction or labelling theory. The elements of such a view are that deviance is seen as a question of social definition. The deviance does not lie in the act but arises when some other person defines that act as deviant. In school-based behaviour this importantly includes teachers. Often the deviant act breaks some rules that may be specific to that culture or community or school. The consequences to the person committing that act often follow from the deviant label which, as we have seen, may be relative to that group or community. This will be explored in our next section where we will look at why, for example, there are more boys than girls in EBD provision.

How you see it makes a difference

There are certain well-trodden teacher explanations for emotional disturbance which need to be examined.

Gender

We start from the observation that there are many more boys than girls in special schools for pupils with EBD. According to McNamara (McNamara and Moreton, 1995) it is not clear what is the causal relationship but there is clearly a connection between teacher attention and types of behaviour. According to Spender (1982) teachers give more attention to boys; boys shout out more and are more aggressive. Teachers give less time to girls; girls tend to conform, chat to each other, and any unhappiness is in the form of withdrawal or anorexia.

Large amounts of verbal abuse and aggressive behaviour are accepted from boys; but small amounts of the same behaviour are stamped on in girls. On the other hand, emotional behaviour accompanied by crying is tolerated in girls whereas it would set alarm bells ringing in boys who, above infant stage, are not expected to show emotion very demonstratively – 'big boys don't cry'.

Race

According to McNamara (McNamara and Moreton, 1995) Afro-Caribbean behaviours are seen as insolent, sly, aggressive, manipulative and non-cooperative, and this may be related to the fact that there are disproportionate numbers of Afro-Caribbean students in schools and units for children with EBD. As they point out 'If teachers were to ask and find out what it is that the Afro-Caribbean pupil is really feeling, they may well find that the motivation, thinking and feeling of this student is actually different to the interpretation placed on it by teachers' (p. 8). This is another example of the need to get inside the cultural meanings of the non-verbal behaviours in order to avoid incorrect labelling with the consequences that flow from that label.

Home background

'What do you expect from that background!' This may indicate that the teacher believes that the behaviour in question is learned and tolerated in the home. It is easy to attribute positive attitudes towards learning and good behaviour to what are considered to be 'good' home backgrounds, and conversely to attribute negative attitudes to children considered to come from 'bad' backgrounds.

This is a sort of 'blanket thinking' about whole patterns of behaviour simply on the basis of one judgement. The teacher's view is conveyed to the pupil through verbal and non-verbal means and may play a part in influencing performance and behaviour, as Rosenthal and Jacobson (1968) have shown.

Teacher attitude

Children who do not meet middle-class expectations may be labelled as deviant. Another way of looking at stroppy working-class boys is to ask whether they are trying to stop the systematic assault on their dignity which constitutes much of secondary school experience, as Hargreaves has argued (Hargreaves, 1982).

This may also may lead to low expectations of such children. *Learning to Labour* is the title given to a book by Paul Willis (Willis, 1977) in which he points out that working-class boys were often denied a broad curriculum. Whether this is so true in these days of entitlement and a National Curriculum is a moot point. On the other side of the coin, teachers expect middle-class children not to show signs of the sort of disturbance that they might excuse in working-class pupils.

Schools can and do make a difference to levels of expulsion/ exclusion and they can change their norms to alter these levels. Sometimes explanations based on social class or pupil motivation need to be challenged.

Blaming or displacing attention away from the school can be exaggerated by the various stereotypical frameworks which teachers use to judge children with EBD. These may lead to a biased view and include social class, home background, gender and race. This is understandable in view of the pressure on teachers to maintain orderly classrooms. It is our intention in this book to look in detail at what classteachers might do in their classes and schools to help children who are emotionally and behaviourally disturbed.

Further we will concentrate on how this might be done in the ordinary school since, as we have shown earlier, the history of this educational field has moved from treatment in special schools towards more educational approaches in ordinary schools.

A starting point

One of the debates which has come back into prominence as a result of this shift has been the relationship between learning and behavioural difficulties. Many of the children with EBD have associated learning difficulties. This provides teachers with a dilemma: do they tackle the behaviour difficulties first?

Getting over the emotional disturbance first and then tackling learning is part of the old medical way but, as experience suggests, this risks not getting round to learning at all. To embrace the challenge of promoting adjustment through the curriculum probably best meets the perceptions of parents, pupils and teachers as to the purpose of school. An important point is that parents and teachers can share the idea that the main function of schools is successful learning of those aspects of knowledge, attitudes and skills which we see as important in our society.

In our view it is a question of balance, and while the old teacher in special schools might have overvalued adjustment before learning, the new philistinism makes the opposite mistake and narrows learning to only academic progress. We will show how the mainstream curriculum should not have a narrow emphasis on academic subjects but should be a broad and balanced curriculum with due attention to personal and social education.

We would argue that, while such a reorganisation is absolutely necessary if we are to cope with children with EBD in the ordinary school, it will also be of benefit to all the other pupils. Indeed, it might be argued that, if this were to take place, the children with EBD might be seen as bringing benefits to the rest of the class in making the school confront these issues and change towards becoming a more humane place for all – an inclusive school where all are welcome and provided for properly. In the light of this argument, we consider that a suitable subtitle for this book might be: 'The gift of the challenging child'. This phrase was suggested to us when the parents of a child arrived for an initial interview with a headteacher known to us. They told the head clearly that their son was challenging, was struggling socially and had several disabilities that frustrated him and led to him irritating others. The head listened and then surprised them by saying, 'He will be a gift to the school'. This child had never had that label put upon him before and his parents were delighted. The boy, although indeed challenging, made great strides in both learning and behaviour in his time at that school.

Chapter 2

The resilient teacher

In this chapter we examine the attitudes necessary for working successfully with other people, both children and adults. We believe that these same attitudes are equally important in dealing with children with emotional and social difficulties. A good teacher of children with EBD will be a good teacher for all children.

The challenge

Let us look at what a good teacher has to cope with. Here are some candid comments from teachers in answer to the question: 'What is the most difficult aspect for you when you have a challenging child in your class?'

> 'I want to share my time between all the children and this child constantly demands a bigger share. It doesn't seem fair to the others.'
> 'Other children can't always hear me or listen carefully to me because this child makes noises or interrupts me. That irritates me.'
> 'This child undermines my authority with the class. I think a teacher needs to feel in control.'
> 'My strategies run out. I lack energy and I don't like having no ideas left to use. I feel as if I'm not a competent teacher when it's like that.'
> 'This child spoils my relationship with the group and I resent that.'
> 'I try hard to build up trust with the child, just as I do with all the children in my class, but this child undermines that trust.

> I feel sabotaged.'
> 'Sheer frustration!'
> 'I know that a child like that will mean extra effort and I'm working flat out as it is.'

These are honest comments from good teachers who, in their own ways, are prepared to tackle the difficulties they meet. They illustrate the view which we expressed in chapter 1 that the unifying feature of EBD is that the children are disturbing to teachers. Whilst some teachers feel a challenge on behalf of the class, others feel a more personal sense of hurt. For this reason, the effectiveness of paying attention to both the teachers' personal process as well as to their grasp of the group process will be argued in this book. In this chapter our stress will be on the personal process of the teacher and we move on to group process in chapter 3.

Let us examine what a good teacher has to cope with given that there are many causes of troubled and troubling behaviour. McNamara and Moreton (1995) see a crucial common feature of children with EBD as having had damaging experiences for reasons such as loss of parents or abusive relationships. They cannot bear any more pain and so erect defences so as not to feel any more. This shutting off makes them non-empathic and thus able, for example, to bully other people without seeming to have any concern for their victim. However, they are also blocked off from praise as well as blame.

A sense of self

One way of understanding what is happening here is self consistency theory. Burns (1982) shows that once a self concept is formed, however good or bad, we will try to protect it. We may even delude ourselves in order to preserve our feelings of self worth. Even a poor self concept is protected lest a worse is formed. In order to defend their self concept, people may go inside themselves and cut themselves off from real communication or, alternatively, display anger and aggression in an attempt to ward off feedback that they fear will make them feel worse. McNamara and Moreton (1995) see 'attention seeking' as also a defence on the assumption that some very needy children have learned that seemingly negative attention is better than none.

What gives us this sense of self in the first place? It is the result of feedback and experience from birth onwards. We know what we are like because others tell us – they give us positive and negative feedback. Coopersmith's research (1967) shows that there are three groups of people who are highly influential in shaping our view of ourselves through giving feedback. These are parents, teachers and peers. Coopersmith found that teachers and peers accounted for two-thirds of the influence and parents a third, especially in academic self-esteem.

Coopersmith (1967) produces evidence that teachers can make a difference to behaviour if they allow and encourage positive and realistic feedback and give it themselves. This will work even against largely negative feedback from elsewhere.

Relationships

To reach such children and help them believe that they are of worth and that they can be different and positive with other people is a real challenge. This is where we feel that improved relationships can make a difference. In this book we look at how good relationships may be fostered at an individual, class and whole-school level. In this chapter, we see skilful teachers working with such children as individuals. In chapter 3 we also, and equally importantly, show you how to build a constructive and cooperative ethos in your class and school by means of fostering personal and social skills through group work. In chapter 4 we look at how other members of staff and other children, as a working community, can help in this venture of reaching out to such children.

Here we concentrate on the attitudes which are helpful to an individual teacher in dealing with children with EBD. We feel this is important since how teachers feel about themselves and their ability to cope in the class is fundamental to what they can achieve. Teachers and their pupils share a common humanity and none of us is immune to attacks on our self-esteem. Thus for the sake of the pupils as well as you as teachers our purpose is to outline the attitudes which we have found useful in working with all children.

One way we like to think about them is that in being a teacher there are two important overlapping roles. That of being a personal tutor and that of being a subject tutor. Sometimes we operate with individual pupils and sometimes with groups, both in our pastoral and subject modes. In our personal tutoring role we might work with an individual in our tutor group to improve his or her relationships with a group while also working with the whole tutor group at the skills of working together. In our subject teaching we are acting in our individual-subject tutoring role while, say, helping a pupil plan a specific assignment. We would be acting in our group-subject tutoring role when helping another class tackle a new sort of task. These examples are drawn from the more compartmentalised world of the secondary school where most teachers have these two roles. In their pastoral role they will be responsible for a tutorial group whom they will get to know well and this will be the vehicle for reaching individual pupils and teaching a group for pastoral purposes. In addition they will be responsible for teaching their subject to a wider range of classes who will themselves all have their own tutor for pastoral purposes. In most primary schools the situation is that the classteacher is responsible for the pastoral dimension of the class as well as most, if not all, of the subject teaching.

However opportunities for building good relationships do have to be created. A problem in many classes of harnessing this approach is that there are few opportunities for open and honest feedback between children as part of their educational experience. The only behaviour allowed is being on task in academic curriculum areas. This has become increasingly common in primary schools as the demands of the National Curriculum grow. More and more attention has to be paid to academic learning with consequently less attention being paid to the personal and social development of the pupils. This has always been a tension in secondary schools but seems to be getting worse across the whole age range in our instrumentally accountable age. This lack of time and opportunity for work in personal and social areas of the curriculum means that pupils lack opportunity to explore issues of personal and social importance together and in doing so, getting to know each other as people. In the absence of these opportunities each child has to guess how they are responded to mainly through non-verbal behaviour. In addition, peers do not come to know the pupil with EBD at a personal level. All they see is behaviour or reputation or the image the pupil is projecting, rather than the real person and so the probability of negative feedback is very high.

It is our belief that good relationships are fundamental to any effective teaching, and that classes where the members are given the skills of working together in social and emotional areas, as well as academic, are good places for all children to be educated. Secure and confident children, used to working cooperatively with other people, are also well able to tackle the academic areas of the curriculum. In addition commerce and industry places a high value on the personal and social skills of employees, and being able to work as a successful member of a team is seen as an important attribute of any job applicant.

Research shows that taking the personal dimension of education seriously in school does lead to better academic achievement. Aspy and Roebuck (1977) summarise work over seventeen years in forty-two states of the USA and in seven other countries. In all they state that they have worked with 2,000 teachers and 20,000 students. Their overall finding is: *students learn more and behave better when they receive high levels of understanding, caring and genuineness, than when they are given low levels of them.*

Let us look in more detail at the 'understanding, caring and genuineness' referred to above. They are based on the lifetime work of the distinguished American psychologist, Carl Rogers. In his inspiring book on education *Freedom to Learn* (1983), Rogers summarises these three key qualities in effective helping and teaching as follows:

> Those attitudes that appear effective in promoting learning can be described. First of all a transparent realness in the facilitator, a willingness to be a person, to be and to live the feelings and thoughts of the moment. When this realness includes a prizing, a trust and a respect for the learner, the climate for learning is enhanced. When it includes a sensitive and accurate empathic listening, then indeed a freeing climate, stimulative of self-initiated learning and growth, exists. The student is trusted to develop.
>
> (Rogers, 1983, p. 133)

Let us look at these in a little more detail.

Realness/genuineness

Rogers writes:

> it is suggested that the teacher can be a real person in her relationships with her students. She can be enthusiastic, can be

> bored, can be interested in students, can be angry, can be sensitive and sympathetic. Because she accepts these feelings as her own, she has no need to impose them on her students. She can like or dislike a student product without implying that it is objectively good or bad or that the student is good or bad. She is simply expressing a feeling for the product, a feeling that exists within herself. Thus she is a person to her students not a faceless embodiment of a curricular requirement nor a sterile tube through which knowledge is passed from one generation to the next. It is obvious that this attitudinal set . . . is sharply in contrast with the tendency of most teachers to show themselves to their pupils simply as roles.
>
> (Rogers, 1983, p. 122)

Prizing, acceptance, non-possessive warmth

Caring, Rogers writes,

> is a caring for the learner but a non-possessive caring. It is an acceptance of this other individual as a separate person having worth in her own right. It is a basic trust – a belief that this other person is somehow fundamentally trustworthy . . . it shows up in a variety of observable ways . . . can be fully acceptant of the fear and hesitation of the student as she approaches a new problem as well as acceptant of the pupil's satisfaction in achievement. Such a teacher can accept the student's occasional apathy . . . personal feelings that both disturb and promote learning – rivalry with a sibling, hatred of authority, concern about personal adequacy. What we are describing is a prizing of the learner as an imperfect human being with many feelings, many potentialities.
>
> (Rogers, 1983, p. 124)

Empathic understanding

'When the teacher', Rogers points out,

> has the ability to understand the student's responses from the inside, has the sensitive awareness of the way the process of education and learning seem to the student, then again the likelihood of significant learning is increased. This kind of under-

> standing is sharply different from the usual evaluative understanding, which follows the pattern of 'I understand what is wrong with you.' When there is a sensitive empathy, however, the reaction in the learner follows something of this pattern 'At last someone understands how it feels and seems to be *me*, without wanting to analyse me or judge me. Now I can grow and learn.'
>
> (Rogers, 1983, p. 125)

We have quoted Rogers's own words at some length to illustrate these core attitudes which he sees as rare and not fully achieved. It may sound like a counsel of perfection but, realistically, developing a little more of these qualities will produce important benefits as shown in the studies by Aspy and Roebuck referred to earlier (Aspy and Roebuck, 1977).

It is evident from work like this that teachers, as individuals, make a difference. We can all recollect positive and negative influences of teachers on our learning about subjects and also about ourselves. We can see that if a teacher is unhappy and has low self-esteem it is likely to make an impact on the children in his or her classes. We know, as teachers, that when things go well we feel involved in our successes and when the situation is difficult it affects us deeply. It is the personal nature of teaching that makes the role both fulfilling and challenging. Nias has looked at teaching as work (Nias, 1989) and concludes that the sense of self to primary school teachers is central to their task. She saw the teachers in her study having substantial selves that were similar in significant ways. 'They thought of themselves as "caring" people (i.e. sometimes as loving, and always as prepared to put the interests of children before their own); people who were concerned to achieve a high standard of occupational competence; people who placed a high value upon autonomy and scope to use their manifold talents; and people who were interested in educational ideas as well as practice' (p. 204).

Teachers and the child with EBD

Let us look at the present position of teachers in relation to children with EBD. Inclusion is a 'buzz word' at the moment and fits in with the belief that we have adopted that all teachers can make a difference, and that the child with EBD is not the realm of the specialist teacher alone. Inclusion, whilst appealing to many teachers' beliefs about democracy, justice and equal opportunity, will also frighten many teachers who feel insufficiently prepared for this task. They are not helped by that modern version of teaching which strips away any responsibility for the personal and social well-being of children with such slogans as 'we're not social workers'. We would argue against such a view but we also recognise this is a genuinely held tenet in some schools. However, a belief in inclusion is worth examining carefully since the underlying attitudes, which are important in teaching children with EBD, are valuable for all children.

Teachers rightly operate from general principles but need to be alert to how these principles may have to be adapted to meet the needs of an individual child. We do not believe that teaching is something where simple answers can be given. Despite the attempts of some people to reduce teaching to a technical process by means of a highly specified curriculum and low-level skills training in 'delivering' such a curriculum, we believe that this is misguided in a profession which, as Nias points out (1989, p. 204), 'places a high value on autonomy and scope to use their manifold talents'. Certainly, this is not the approach adopted in this book, and we see the reality of teaching as having to cope on a daily level with questions such as how to provide enough structure to make the situation sufficiently safe for learning yet without being so rigid that creativity and flexibility is stifled. There is no one right answer. It will vary from individual to individual, class to class and from day to day. The teacher continually seeks balance – 'Should I focus on this child or that, on this work or that?' Everything cannot be done at once so focusing on particular areas is necessary, but with one eye open for all those other potential priorities hovering around and waiting to land. It is this complexity that is both a challenge and a gift. Teaching has within it certain general skills that can be honed, together with a knowledge base, but we also recognise that there is an intuitive element that allows teachers to work with subtle details which are harder to pin down. These elements are more difficult to share and we will do this by means of our case studies which, we hope, will 'speak' to teachers and allow them to appreciate the subtleties of working with children with EBD.

The following case study shows how a teacher was challenged by children in her class.

Challenging children

I have been severely challenged by two children and must own my part in those interactions. One child was physically such a bully to his peers and so physical and uncaring that I was hurt and defensive on their behalf. I am frightened by physical violence and crumple up inside if I have to witness it on television, let alone in real life. I admit that his continuous attacks on children I cared for wore me down and I had to fight against my own instincts to dislike this needy child. He pushed away my help and ignored or did not notice my generosity towards him, and I struggled with myself for a prolonged period. I know that I have a particularly well-developed flight reflex in such circumstances and it was having to steel myself to stay and watch calculated hurt that took it out of me. I had to keep pushing away a protective mechanism that wanted to perceive this child as not worthy of my help and deserving of exclusion. I needed to give myself a rest from him. I hadn't enough reserves to keep facing him and keep on being fair to him. The fact that I did fight off the feelings crowding in on me was luck rather than resourcefulness – he began to respond and to alter just enough to restore a little of my confidence and I crawled back up the ladder of managing myself in the situation.

The other case was a child with very little sense of his own identity who pushed away every single approach I made to build up a relationship with him. Again, I own in myself a lack of confidence in relationships and recognise that I do not push myself on to those who do not seem immediately receptive. I have to see some sign that I am wanted before I risk a personal investment in all types of relationships and it is the same with children in my class. This boy pushed away my outstretched hand so many times and sabotaged so many efforts to accept him as a valued member of the class that I wanted truly to give up and let someone else give him what he needed. This was compounded by the fact that all class members whom I also cared for had been pushed away and emotionally trampled upon, and I hurt to see their distress. He was not any less deserving of being given a chance but he had personally challenged me emotionally and I began to recognise that I would not be fair to him anymore. I reached a point of total emotional exhaustion along with the class and had to appeal to a colleague to take the class in order to allow me to recharge my batteries and to rethink my approach. I needed a different perception of the problem. I also had to help the class with their perception of the problem. Both children, as a result of their own damage and low self-esteem, had learned early on to live up to expectations. They were adept at pressing the right buttons to elicit the response in an adult that I was also feeling. They were used to fitting adult perceptions that they were difficult. In order to come out unscathed and with no additional effort I could have put the blame on them and wiped my hands of them but I had to own my own part in the difficulties. I had to change my perception and interpret in a different way.

In retrospect, I think that I would have got to know these children for themselves much more quickly if I had made better sense of the emotional muddle I found myself in. With the luxury of distance I can now see more of the jigsaw and I can take stock of how far I have come in my own personal development. I have become more familiar with the process of saying what is mine and what truly belongs with the child. I can more readily see the positives which are there to be brought to the surface, and I am more economical with the steps I take to get to know the core of this child, rather than his behaviours or his label.

However tempting it may be to see myself as amateur then, I intend to be respectful of where I was when each of these children was in my class. It would be easy with hindsight to dismiss my genuine efforts to include them among their classmates. The truth is that I did the best that I knew how, and I believe that I did make a difference to the way things were in school for them. I lit a few candles for them and for me. But what is being a teacher if it is not being a learner too?

Somewhere along the line I find ways of reflecting back to the child how I came back and coped. I believe that children who get themselves into a downwards spiral with adults often frighten them off so they have no useful feedback from the very people who could access their emotional growth.

I have to get back to that child as a valuable person with a host of gifts to offer rather than a major irritant who winds everybody up so that they cannot see clearly or even want to bother. I have to turn the tables; add the element of surprise; face the difficulties and not be overwhelmed by them.

Yes, I have taken care of the emotions triggered in me and have acknowledged my upset, irritation, anger, frustration, but I have not lost sight of the child for who he is.

A similar struggle was recorded forty years ago by David Wills who wrote:

> It is said that one cannot switch affection on and off like an electric current and indeed one cannot; but one can get much nearer to it than is commonly supposed. I find that if one behaves towards a child as if one were fond of him – if one goes, so to speak, through the motions – one's behaviour, at first the result of deliberate volition, becomes in a very short time charged with real affect and one finds that one is really fond of the child for whom previously one had been merely pretending affection.
>
> (Wills, 1960, p. 38)

He goes on to describe the mystics loving God through an act of the will and then quotes the Bible saying how much easier it is to love our brother whom we have seen than God who we have not seen:

> But perhaps there is a fallacy in this argument. It may be just because we have seen our brother that we find it difficult to love him. We may not be able to see God but neither can we smell Him, and we can smell our brother. He stinks because he soils his pants, he kicks us in the shins and repays any kindness with abuse. How can one love such a creature?
>
> It is quite easy if the will is there; not easy – simple. One merely decides that one will do so and acts towards one's beastly brother as if one did love him. It is as simple, and as difficult as that, although of course it must be accompanied by a sympathetic understanding. If one perseveres one finds in time that one is acquiring a genuine feeling of affection for the child.
>
> (Wills, 1960, p. 45)

Personal attitudes

Let us now look at how a teacher might give attention to his/her own attitudes when confronted with a child with EBD. We suggest that teachers should really pay attention to their perspectives at this initial stage. We encourage them to ask lots of questions of themselves about the child, about what they are doing and how the class, including themselves and the new child, are responding to each other.

Points to reflect on

What do I like about this child?
What is he good at?
Am I frightened by this child?
Am I looking at this child or his label/history?
Can I offer what he needs on my own?
How can I handle my feelings if he irritates me etc.?
How do I usually talk to him?
What sort of interactions does he have with adults?
What sort of interactions does he have with his own peer group?
Who does he get along best with and why?

We feel it is important for teachers to recognise emotions that they are feeling and to see if they can identify their source. Are they coming from old hurts and insecurities and is this reaction to a child more to do with this history than to the actual behaviour of the child concerned? Challenging children highlight sides of teachers with which they feel uncomfortable. It is important that teachers are aware of and 'own' their emotions. Such emotions, as well as prejudices, come to the fore when people are challenged. We believe that, if teachers are in a supportive environment, these emotions and prejudices can be worked on. In this way, such children can actually enable teachers to develop personally. These seemingly negative experiences can then be seen as an opportunity if teachers are willing to engage with these personally difficult areas. As Wahl puts it: 'this work has been a fast track to personal development. The intensity of the experiences I have had with these children has taught me in ten years what may otherwise have taken a lifetime or two' (Wahl, 1999).

This emotional engagement with the process of teaching means that much is at stake and criticism of one's work is hard to take. The positive side to this two-edged process is that successes, when celebrated, allow us opportunities to raise our own self-esteem and that difficulties, when faced, allow us opportunities for learning about ourselves. Teaching also allows us the chance to develop our interests and to enthuse children about these. Similarly it gives us scope for accepting that we have weaknesses. In our experience these areas of weakness can be turned to good effect by, for example, allowing children to see us struggling with a musical instrument and allowing them to help us to make improvements. This shows one of our basic principles which is that it is helpful for the teacher to involve the children in all learning. A teacher's willingness to accept ideas from children and understand and accept their viewpoint, enables them to see things differently. This can be a huge release for teachers who may at times be over-responsible trying to sort out and improve every last dimension of their classrooms. Groups of children when confronted with challenging behaviour are extremely adept at offering ideas if encouraged to do so. As we shall see in detail in the next chapter, it is often so much more effective and rewarding when a child is challenging you or others in the group to ask the children what we can do about this. The children's ownership of strategies also improves the likelihood of success.

We have already looked at the fundamental qualities of genuineness, non-possessive warmth and empathic understanding detailed by Rogers. Linked to this genuiness is an honesty in relation to self and to others. The teacher does not hide behind a role but is authentic and consistent both with colleagues and children. This requires the teacher to understand him/herself including his/her less attractive sides. This helps teachers to own their own difficult feelings and not to project them on to the children, especially when such children are often good at picking up on areas of weakness and insecurity in teachers. This is linked to a non-blaming approach where the teacher tries to stay positive and offer ways for children to find solutions. It may be that talking with sympathetic colleagues is helpful in understanding ourselves and in allowing our difficult feelings to be discharged.

Threats from the outside

We all carry our own expectations that originate from the school, the outside world and ourselves. Teachers are often a target when things go wrong. They are told that education should do this or that and that standards have dropped here or there. This is not to say there are no weaknesses, but we feel that the strengths of such a dedicated profession are often unsung. The climate this creates is often one of blame and we should therefore not be surprised when this spills out in other directions. Frequently blame is directed towards the challenging child or the parents of this child. Statements such as 'It would be so different if Wayne or Waynetta were not in this class' are frequent. Whilst it is understandable that teachers feel annoyed when challenged, they need to ask themselves whether it is helpful to blame either the parents or the child.

What is needed is courage, although having courage does not prevent us from feeling anxious or fearful. Often, where a child carries a label, we are half expecting trouble. We need to recognise that, by changing our perception of the child, it may be possible to influence events positively and prevent the appearance of the undesired behaviour. We would then be more likely to give equal opportunities, trust and positive responses to the child concerned.

Fear and worry seem to be the major factors building up negative and downward spirals which can lead to an atmosphere in a school in which the exclusion of the child can be contemplated as a solution. These factors lead to blame and make problem-solving more difficult. In a blame-ridden environment the problem is more likely to be seen as the child's, or the inadequate teacher's, or the fault of 'those parents'. This is illustrated by Emilia Dowling in an example where:

> A secondary school requested that 'something must be done' with a boy who was described as severely disturbed. When teachers were asked for a specific example of how he behaved and what made him appear as severely disturbed, they referred to the fact that he punched a boy who had accidentally knocked his lunch tray and spilt milk on his blazer. This was, the head of year said, the proof of how severely disturbed he was – a disproportionate reaction to a relatively minor incident. The head had chosen to punctuate reality at the point of the boy's behaviour, labelling it as disturbed. Exploration of the context revealed that the mother, a widow living on Social Security, had saved for a year to buy George a new blazer and had threatened to 'beat the hell out of him' if he damaged it. This was the first time George had worn his blazer.
>
> (Dowling and Osborne, 1994, pp. 5–6)

In the quote above, the head is described as punctuating reality at the point of the boy's behaviour. As Dowling goes on to point out 'no punctuation is right or wrong – it just reflects a view of reality' (Dowling and Osborne, 1994, p. 6).

When the view is taken that nobody should be seen to be blamed and all are seen as supported, everyone, including the child, is more likely to move from entrenched positions. If things go wrong in this more flexible environment, people are likely to learn from it and move on positively.

When teachers state all children or adults 'have to', 'should', 'must', then things are more likely to break down. This is not to say that high expectations are not held or that boundaries are not in place but that these boundaries are realistic and match where the child is developmentally.

At times, particularly when we are less confident of, say, the curriculum content or school environment, we are likely to plan more. When working with a child with EBD it is tempting, when we have spent time planning, to not let the challenging child 'spoil' our efforts. Similarly such a child may limit our willingness to take risks. However, it is often these risks which can shift the way we work with such a child. It is helpful to remember that the uncertainty one experiences may be exactly how the child feels when he or she embarks on a new learning experience. At such times we have the opportunity to model for the child the process of facing up to difficulties. If we allow the class to know that we are feeling nervous or unsure then, in our experience, the class is likely to respond very positively to such honesty.

When things are difficult it is tempting for people either to pretend they have an answer or to avoid the task completely. If we do this we model, for children, the belief that it is important always to be right and that getting it right is vital. When the environment allows for uncertainty people, both children and adults, are freed up to acknowledge that they don't know and then everyone's level of creativity can increase. Complex issues naturally produce uncertainties. Quite often, in our experience, the process of naming the 'not knowing' allows the situation to change without anything else needing to be done other than providing the assurance that the adults are going to help everyone stick with it and look for ways forward.

In these challenging situations there are certain ideas which may be helpful for teachers to remember. Firstly, it takes time to change behaviour. We should remind ourselves how difficult it may have been for us to do something such as giving up chocolate or stopping smoking. It is easy to assume that a child can change if they want to but we need to remember that often there is much at stake and that the child needs our support and that of his or her peers. We may need to mobilise help from the rest of the group and the school in order to effect such change. This will be covered in chapters 3 and 4.

An awareness of our own internal thought processes is valuable and is perhaps most heightened following experiences where we have had to engage as the learner, perhaps on a residential course, being asked to do things that we frequently ask children to do. We would recommend that teachers seek out opportunities for inservice training in group-work methods. The difficulty of getting into a group or working with someone who isn't your first choice reminds us of what it is like to be in the children's shoes. The week following such experiences we will certainly be more sensitive to children's needs. It therefore seems vital that we engage, on a regular basis, with such training as part of our Inset programme.

Meeting personal needs

Given the importance we have placed on our own internal processes in providing a helpful way of viewing the child with EBD, it should not come as a surprise that we also place importance on the teacher looking after him- or herself. Our own experience is that teachers work extremely hard and it follows that they have a need to look after themselves. This includes the drawing of boundaries in a job where there are always endless things to do. When teachers are under pressure it is tempting to see the dedicated professional as someone who says 'I'll show you that I work hard' and puts in even more time and effort. We believe that we need to struggle but also to allow ourselves to recharge. We suggest that you sometimes write down your problems and thus place them 'outside' yourself or visualise leaving your worries in a certain place on the way back from work. They'll still be waiting for you in the morning!

Looking after ourselves is rarely promoted when training as a teacher but it's a key to our success. Everyone finds his or her own ways of unwinding. For some it will be an emotionally satisfying activity such as playing the piano, reading or sitting in the garden. For others, it will be physical activity. Research finds that teachers who keep themselves physically fit have the necessary stamina to get through a busy teaching week (see Buhler and Aspy, 1975). We suggest that each teacher finds his/her way of keeping fit whether by going to the gym for a good workout, taking part in team sports, going for a long hike, or just taking the dog for a walk on a regular basis.

Our thoughts are affected by the class we work with, by our own personal history and by the parents and communities with whom we work. Whilst it is important for us to recognise that we can make a difference, it is also realistic to recognise the stresses and support that come from elsewhere. We need to acquire the skill of balancing all these various influences. Sometimes we flounder, occasionally we strike oil and experience the feeling that this is what we were after, only for the balance to move again and for the struggle to be renewed.

Points to reflect on

How do I look after myself/unwind?
Can I improve my time management?
How do I keep emotionally fit?
How do I keep physically fit?
Do I celebrate my good days?

We know that we need to respond and process large amounts of information as we are working in the classroom. We make mistakes and have successes but we feel the balance is more productive when we are allowed (or allow ourselves) the space to make decisions based on what feels the correct professional choice. This approach is far from easy to pin down and yet, for us, it is rigorous, hard work. There is not one correct solution. What we need to do is to build on the abilities that our class and we have already developed.

The following case study illustrates the subtleties of working with children with EBD. In this study one of the authors reflects on the idea of inclusion and exclusion by examining how a child who is initially seen as included in a school becomes a suitable case for exclusion.

What's happening to Graham?

The perception held by our school community at one time was that Graham was OK in school. He had extreme needs; was developmentally young for his age; had inadequate social skills, but was a loveable and often loving boy aged five years who had already been excluded from one school but whom we felt deserved a chance to learn alongside his mainstream peers. He began to develop a good relationship with one or two adults, and would spend a lot of time in the classroom and a little outside playing with his learning support assistant (LSA). Staff were indeed becoming aware of him and were interpreting and understanding him by observing his actions and by interacting with him. There were memories of good and bad times with Graham. He was a boy who was developing amongst staff and children – 'This is Graham. This is what he can do. This is what he has learned. This is what he needs to do to develop further.'

The school underwent many changes of staff including the head teacher and Graham is no longer perceived as he was. I see his classteacher driven to distraction by his behaviour and bellowing at him that she doesn't really care and will not have him doing what he does any more. I see a case conference where the head is advising a change for Graham – to be better for him – a fresh start in a more appropriate setting. 'After all, we have done all we can for him and it is up to him now.'

What has happened to change the approach to this boy? From inclusion and a feeling of forward movement and progress towards a future goal, to exclusion and a feeling that the end of the road has been reached and there is no more looking forward – no more process of 'becoming' and 'understanding'. That open-ended ongoing process or 'interpreting' and building up a memory bank seems to have gone from the equation, and things are blocked, closed, non-negotiable, finished.

Has the child done something totally dreadful? Has he changed overnight? Has he been open to some awful new influence that has altered him beyond belief? As an outsider to the class I see him around school exactly as I saw him before. He's doing more or less the same things and being Graham – a complicated and damaged six-year-old. His classteacher and LSA have changed but he has taken the changes in his stride and he is still with the peer group he started with. He's a little taller and his peers are achieving a lot more than him academically but the differences are not great. In fact, he now has a little more LSA time covering his statement of special educational needs and has become a little more socially aware at playtimes.

The fact is that if we are personally 'in tune' with a child, the child prospers. If we are personally threatened or undermined by being with a child, the child does not flourish. If our emotions are triggered by something a child does, it is difficult to think of the child in his own context anymore. We might remember something from our childhood – an old injustice or hurt, a character from school days, a parent, etc. What chance has the child then of being seen in his own light?

Once an adult feels threatened, undermined, unsupported, unconfident around a difficult child, things rarely get easier. The dynamic between teacher and class can rapidly shift if the adult is under par. It is a job where you just have to be a hundred per cent. If one child unwittingly or with intent triggers off a response of fear, anger, insecurity or irritation in the teacher, the teacher's perception of the child may change – he is now a challenge or a threat to success. The teacher can be worried about seeming to be ineffectual in front of the class, Children are quick to gang up and further add to the teacher's insecurity and difficulty.

At this point I'd like to use an image outside teaching of how a big difference can be created in the way something is thought about by adults, by the way those adults act. It is along the lines of 'Don't panic Mr Mainwaring' from the TV show *Dad's Army*.

We have a first aider who knows his stuff but lacks any sensitivity towards the casualty. He receives an injured child from the playground with a twisted leg. He talks loudly and in an agitated manner, sitting the child down on his own whilst he stands above it. Basically he picks up the child's distress and panics!

'Broken leg. Yes you may have a broken leg there. I'm going to check it out.' 'Broken leg?' thinks the child – worst possible scenario! 'Just relax now I'm going to move your leg to see whether it is broken', booms the first aider.

The child has presented with a possible broken leg and the first aider has bought that into perception. He has fuelled that view and is panicking along with the child. Stress levels are rising and the situation is serious and has to be approached with a heavy brow and a determined voice. The casualty, already in shock, gives up all hope of things getting better and becomes difficult and awkward. Now the first aider has a really exhausting and difficult job on his hands! This is a difficult case!

I think of our other first aider who greets the casualty with a smile and a bit of a joke and offers a reassuring arm around the shoulders. She talks quietly about sorting things out and invites the child to talk about what happened and when, before even focusing on the injury. What does the child want and need? All the time she is casting her eye over the possible broken leg and keeping her thoughts in her head. Together they sort of flow smoothly into looking at the leg and easing the panicky feelings. The child gets a little control back and is part of the forward progress they make in sorting out the problem. The leg is not broken in either case. The perception is very different, however.

First aider A: 'You present a broken leg: I perceive that you have a broken leg and I will treat the leg'.

First aider B: 'You present a broken leg: I want to find out if you have a broken leg. You may not have one. I can see that you need some comfort and reassurance and you are still capable of being you even if you do have a broken leg.

Child: 'But I always have a broken leg. It's my leg adults always look at and fuss over. They know what to do about my leg, they respond straight away to my leg – I am a leg!'

'I am a broken leg = I am a disruptive child. QED.

Let us take these thoughts back to Graham in school. 'We've done all we can for him and it's up to him now. He knows the positive reward system here. He knows what he has to do to earn approval, and if he behaves negatively he knows by now that he gets sent home.'

'Graham is broken leg.' That is the commonly held perception of him at school now. And in a way he cannot get it right. If he can sometimes pretend his leg is not broken then he is rewarded. If he moans about his broken leg, he gets excluded. Has he even got a broken leg? Is there more to him than that? Has his problem become everything there is about him now? Is he his own label?

Most of the things the staff reflect back to him are negative: 'I don't like it when you do that.' 'No.' 'Well done for managing five minutes at register time but don't do this again'. He *is* exhausting. He *is* irritating. He *is* driving everyone mad and he *is* personally challenging. And his teacher is not in any way wrong. She is at the end of her patience and ingenuity. She has given her all. She has done so much to try to include him in her class. She has really bent over backwards.

The head has a duty to support and protect her in a supervisory role. And there are other children in her class who have a right to learn and be left in peace. The head is not wrong. She is acting responsibly and will take the final decision that enough is enough for all concerned. They all set out this year with good intentions and a liking for this child but it has gone sour on them.

I hear the classteacher complaining that Graham is rude and insolent to her, and if there is one thing she can't take it is rudeness

> from someone she is trying to be kind to and help. That teacher has it in her to own her feelings and could explore just how much is actually Graham and how much is Graham triggering off some historical emotions in her. She is only a thought or two away from understanding more about herself and her perception of Graham. She is only a step away from reframing some of her negative thoughts so that she can 'translate', using a different word, and in so doing shift the understanding of something that Graham has done. She is a good teacher who has been personally challenged and she could go either way. We all draw the line somewhere and she is very close to reaching for a metaphorical pen and ruler.

Here we see a reference to 'reframing', which is giving a new frame or meaning to a situation 'which fits the "facts" of the same concrete situation equally, or even better and thereby changes its entire meaning' (Watzlawick *et al.*, 1974, p. 95). For example, when a child runs out of class when an argument has blown up, it may be possible to reframe their actions as positive for avoiding getting into a fight rather than tell them off for running away. It is helpful for the child if the teacher verbally acknowledges understanding of his action. It also allows the adult to build on the next step through a statement such as 'next time you need to run away from something difficult can you go to such and such a place?' This approach can ultimately lead the child, to being able to face up to such difficult situations within the class without running away.

Reframing can help when it is difficult to stay positive when faced with challenges. The belief that 'blaming others results in things becoming stuck' may help a teacher avoid blaming others but this does not necessarily help them to deal with their own feelings about the situation. It is not about pretending that everything is OK but it is about acknowledging that somewhere there is something positive that will enable steps forward to be taken. Seemingly negative situations may eventually provide opportunities for learning.

At times the last thing you may feel you want to do is look for something positive in a situation but this ability to reframe is very important if we are to stay focused on finding solutions and not get drawn into the problem ourselves. When a parent comes in angrily then it can be helpful to reframe her anger as highlighting her child's importance to her. It doesn't make the difficulty vanish but it allows you the opportunity to react non-defensively to what you might have interpreted as their hostility and aggression towards you.

However, the struggle involved means that a teacher needs support and in the final section of the case study the author reflects on where she looks for support.

Who can you turn to?

What can help a teacher after a hard day with a challenging child? The plain fact is that no one can know how isolating it is to feel out of control as a teacher in a class. Who can you turn to? If you confide in a colleague you risk losing your professional confidence and competence because they don't find the child a problem. If you risk all with your head or year head they will feel obliged to watch you more closely in a supervisory role and disempower you further, however helpful they may want to be. If you confide in a partner at home you are usually talking to a supportive but unknowing buddy who may not really get to the root of things. After all, your perspective of the child at that difficult time will probably coax them to see the child as you do, and you can do no more than wallow about in self-condolences. If you seek a buddy in a teacher from another school, you usually find they have experienced similar episodes and have no professional agenda with you when offering their advice.

Teachers risk a lot when they ask for help and open themselves up to the help and advice from others. Everyone means well, but when catapulted into the role of helpful buddy how many of us jump at the chance to be the expert, the problem solver, in our enthusiasm to fix it quick?

The most helpful buddies I have are those who throw the problem back to me and encourage me to dig deep into my own knowledge of how to be with children. They really listen as I thrash about in my own confusion, exploring one aspect and then another, then pulling myself apart, then the child. What they do is to reflect back to me what it is I am doing, and ask me why I think I'm doing it. They hear the positive bits, they see the tiniest strengths and they hold them up for me to acknowledge. When I have managed to see again the positive connection with this child it almost takes on its own energy and things start to happen. I know what it is. With that embryonic positive feeling about the child, I go back to class and somehow the child notices it, and I get some payback.

> Maybe I say something in a different way or I allow some action or recognise a result. It's at a very obvious level to the child, I believe, although the class may not see it. Whatever it is, the two of us know that there has been a shift in my perception and it becomes a two-way channel for communication.

Conclusion

In this chapter we have explored some of the key attitudes necessary for working successfully with adults and children. We have stated that a good teacher of children with EBD will be a good teacher for all children. In looking at our own practice in the classroom we need to be aware of the qualities we value as individuals; the behaviours that we model; the types of feedback that we give and allow and the way that we reflect and reframe. If we are alert to the way we operate as teachers, before we have to face a challenge, then we may be better equipped to be pro-active rather than re-active. What is needed is courage and a willingness to engage as a learner.

Chapter 3

Creating an inclusive classroom

This chapter outlines some of the strategies that teachers can draw upon to manage the classroom context to support the children who challenge the teacher and/or the group. We begin by looking at the way that group work can be used to build community and inclusivity within the classroom and also can be used to manage the challenging situations that teaching so often delivers. Whilst we use a group-work approach, the ideas described do not have to be used in such a manner. Good teaching is about adapting ideas and making them your own. We recognise that there are not set prescriptive answers such as if *A* happens do *B*. The ideas developed here are not only those suitable for specialist teachers of children with EBD, but are sound educational practice that will enable all children to move forward positively.

The management of the classroom from resources to layout to ethos and teaching styles is important. It relies on those attitudes which we looked at in the last chapter, and which inform our judgement to choose wisely among the range of skills we possess for a given situation. We recognise that it can be easy to become stuck in using certain strategies whilst neglecting others. This chapter will demonstrate how classroom management techniques can be knitted together to produce a consistent approach using group-work processes. No set strategy will always be sufficient for every situation, but the processes described here are very general since they are about building and using the classroom community to gain consensus and involve everyone in looking for solutions. We saw a similar approach in chapter 2 where we suggested that the teacher builds a relationship with an individual child and then works through the relationship to help the child deal with his or her emotional and behavioural difficulties. In addition, while some hold the view that the best form of education is at an individual level, we take the view that there are also important personal and social gains to be made for children by the experience of living and working in that particular environment we call the class. The class we refer to is the main unit of the primary school while in the secondary school we describe the groupings of young people that form the focus for pastoral care in a school.

Most secondary schools are too big and specialised for the pupils to stay together in any one group. However, most have adopted some organisational arrangement whereby each pupil is in a group where one member of staff can get to know him or her well. This is often called the tutorial group and is the group where an individual member of staff exercises that part of their tutoring role that we have called personal tutoring in chapter 2. In this role each tutor is responsible for the individual well-being of each pupil. There is another broad part to the role and that is work with the whole tutor group. Many secondary schools locate that part of the curriculum to do with personal and social education to the time when this group meets with their tutor. The goals of such a period might be defined as providing a context and structure through which pupils can have the opportunity to develop and extend on themes they find important and which influence progress at school. They do this through examining the real influences on their lives, without avoiding the difficult processes and feelings, and with a clear focus on action and on the particular strategies to apply. They investigate these issues in their contexts – school, home and community. This emphasis on the particular makes them an ideal place in which to consider such questions as how the group can help an individual who has EBD to cope better and make the most of their schooling.

In the primary school this personal tutoring role will be taken by the classteacher but the content and approach will be similar. To help teachers with this classroom dimension we will look at the knowledge and skills necessary for a teacher to create a cooperative ethos in the group. Although it is important for the teacher to understand and be familiar with group-work, opportunities need to be found for the class to understand and practise these ideas as well. The reason for paying attention to them here is that they provide the context in which the child with EBD will be integrated. We firmly believe that the class is a vital resource in our efforts to help these children as well as providing a context in which all the children can gain in personal and social ways. Finally we also believe that a well-functioning class will be able to achieve academically since social and personal progress are interlinked with academic work at both primary and secondary phases.

In this chapter we refer several times to group work and we will explain at this point what we mean by a group and how groups of various sizes are important in education, and how an understanding of group dynamics can help teachers be effective in their class teaching. We draw extensively in this section on the work of Watkins and Thacker in their book on tutoring (Watkins and Thacker, 1993). First of all there is the class as a whole and this is usually a big group of between twenty to thirty plus. The teacher also works with smaller groups on occasion that may be formed from within the class group. The use of small groups in the classroom can give rise to a number of misunderstandings and we need to be clear about what they are about.

Use of small groups

The first classification is working *in* groups. This can refer to a minimal but important version of classroom organisation – the grouping of tables and chairs. At a minimum, pupils may find themselves doing individual tasks round a single table. As the Plowden Report (Plowden, 1967) pointed out, only seven or eight minutes a day would be available for each child if all teaching were individual. Sharing out the teacher's time is therefore a major problem and Plowden recommended that teachers therefore have to economise by teaching together a small group of children who are working at the same stage.

In essence, the children are doing individual work, and communication (if any) between pupils could be about anything. Bennett (1987) confirmed that this is a common feature of the primary classroom and was critical of the lack of genuine group tasks with the result that any contact between the pupils was unplanned and could even be counterproductive because no two children were working on the same aspect of a task. Often this use of the small group can encourage the formation of cliques within the classroom – e.g. 'we're the top group', 'we're the special-needs group' – and promote attitudes that prevent an easy working relationship with everyone in the group. Hence it is common to find scapegoating of a group member who is slightly different, or boys and girls preferring not to work together, or one group feeling superior to another.

As a result of this, children can often find working *in* groups a haphazard and unsystematic experience. Collaboration takes place only within clearly defined limits usually involving one's friends. However, life does not allow us to interact only with people we like. School is a microcosm of society and as such is both a reality in itself and a preparation for the adult world. We need to help children work successfully with a range of people, not just their friends. As we shall see, this is an important emphasis in our approach, particularly as we want to use groups as a way of integrating pupils with EBD.

A more sophisticated use is that of work *as* groups. This requires that the task demands of a group of pupils that they contribute to the achievement of some overall objective. This may mean the contribution of differing perspectives, the adoption of particular allocated roles and so on. This is the hallmark of classroom cooperation, enterprise projects, etc. Such a use of groups has the benefits listed in the box.

Groups:

1. Offer increased communication and engagement about a learning task.
2. Can recognise and enhance the social processes that support learning – communicating, accommodating new ideas, explaining, applying ideas.
3. Can offer a range of ideas and perspectives and can be used to gather perspectives, examine their differences.
4. Can become supportive places, including for learning, looking at study approaches, using each other as resources.
5. Demand the use of communication skills – listening, perspective-taking, understanding others, communicating points of view.
6. Demand collaboration on some occasions or some tasks.
7. Demand group processes when faced with problems to solve.
8. Demand skills of identifying and making decisions.

As Hopson and Scally (1981) say: 'Perhaps if one were to identify the one skill most crucial for individuals to develop, for many it would be how to be effective in the groups in which we live, play and work . . . That skill is likely to be best learned by operating regularly as a member of actual groups, as a part of the educational process' (p. 112).

The final use of groups we want to pick out is learning *about* groups. This refers to the occasions when working as groups is developed into a learning process about groups themselves. Pupils take time to explicitly address the workings of the group in a structured way, and an increasing self-awareness of group functioning is promoted.

Groups:

1. May be used to simulate social processes that occur elsewhere.
2. May provide a platform for preparing for other group experiences, outside the group, in the future.
3. May provide a context for reflecting on our own performance.
4. May provide opportunities for people to give and receive personal feedback.
5. May become safe contexts for supporting growth and experiment.

It is this use of groups that we are stressing in this pastoral side of classroom life and this is in the spirit of Leslie Button who says that:

> Group work is about helping people in their social skills, in their personal resource and in the kind of relationships they establish with other people. Social skills can be learnt only in contact with other people, and it is the purpose of group work to provide the individual with opportunities to relate to others in a supportive atmosphere, to try new approaches and to experiment in new roles.
>
> (Button, 1974, p. 1)

It is primarily this use of groups that we are talking about in this chapter. We will show how using groups in this way helps the teacher to gain the support of the rest of the class in the inclusion of a child with EBD.

Such small support groups might be a regular part of the tutor sessions in the secondary school. In the primary class, the children have longer with the teacher and are developmentally less reliant on relationships with peers for their personal and social needs.

This is not to say that at either primary or secondary level there is an exclusive focus on small groups. The structure always follows the intention for the session. At both primary and secondary school stages the teacher needs a similar range of knowledge and skills. For example, when communicating classroom routines, a whole-class approach is most appropriate while a small-group approach would be appropriate for carrying out some research and presenting it to the whole class. On the other hand, an individual approach may be necessary to help a pupil to complete a Record of Personal Achievement.

Since the 1960s it has become fashionable to place primary-aged children in groups around tables even when they may be doing individual work. By doing so we almost invite the children to chat about concerns extraneous to the task set. Consider whether or not it may be better to place the class in rows or with the tables arranged so that the children are not distracted.

However, if you do want children to discuss their work as part of a cooperative assignment, then the tables can be moved into groups facing each other. On occasion, where the whole class is working as a group, the whole classroom should be rearranged so that the class can sit in a circle where everyone can see everybody else. Not only does this 'speak' of the fact that we are all present here as equals, it also means that each person can see and be seen when they want to speak. Sometimes it is necessary to break the large group into smaller groups and this can be arranged, on a temporary basis, with the smaller groups returning eventually to the large-circle formation. Furniture-shifting is a way of life in our approach! We have found that giving the children the task of clearing a space and putting out a circle of chairs for everyone to sit on can be a valuable group-learning task in itself. Resisting the temptation to select a few sensible members of the group to 'get it ready for everyone' can be difficult at first but we suggest that you give this task to the whole group and make sense of what you see happening. There will be those who quickly get their own chair and their own space; those who organise everyone around them; those who wait for it to be done for them; those who watch and take what is left. An invitation to the finally seated individuals to say how they went about the task and, perhaps, how they felt, how they thought they might do it another time and what they thought they did well. Such questions will throw up some interesting observations. Encouraging those individuals who choose to give this feedback to always use 'I . . .' statements will serve to model for the group a culture of 'no blame' but of individual ownership.

Focusing on group work as a specific topic, rather than just assuming knowledge of groups, helps people understand what makes groups work, or not work. This knowledge allows participants to play their part in making them function more effectively. It helps the individual members of the group to understand more about themselves and how they feel, act, react and respond to the world in which they find themselves. Often people have no problems with working in groups until the individual or the group suffers some sort of breakdown. Then it may not be clear what went wrong or how to put it right, so those in the group may end up feeling dissatisfied or the group may even fall apart. Problematic groups are familiar to us all and we may only need to look as far as our regular staff meetings to find an example. When a staff group is not functioning well, even relatively straightforward tasks can meet with unsurmountable obstacles. Those long and heated meetings when things still aren't decided ring bells with many of us. Talking about the staff Christmas get-together might, at a surface level, appear to be about What we're going to do, When we are going to do it and Where. When we become aware of group process however, we start to notice so much more.

By giving people the opportunity to develop group work skills we are enabling them both to be able to diagnose a situation and to intervene for a positive outcome. This allows action to be taken to move a group beset with cliques and rivalries towards one characterised by mutual acceptance, support and care.

Points to reflect on

In my staff group:

Do I listen to others without interrupting?
What do I contribute to the group?
Am I listened to?
When the group has a problem, how do I respond?
How do I communicate my point of view?

Stages of group development

Let us consider the kinds of group dynamics through which a class moves over an academic year. During this time a teacher may talk of the children being unnaturally quiet at the start; squabbling a lot; working well; being difficult to handle at the end of the year and so on. These are everyday ways of speaking about the inevitable stages the group needs to go through as it learns to work together. One version of the stages of group development is that of Tuckman (1965) who lists them as 'forming, storming, norming, and performing' to which he later added the idea of 'adjourning' (Tuckman and Jensen, 1977). The studies on which Tuckman based his sequence used adult groups in which there were non-directive leaders who made no attempt to intervene in the group process. In schools there is usually a more interventional style of leadership by an adult in a child group, and we suggest that the order, forming, norming, storming, performing and adjourning, is more appropriate in a classroom context and is the order we will use in this chapter. In the following sections we examine each of these stages as we show you how we build a cooperative community in our classrooms.

Building an inclusive and cooperative community

Group work is a very helpful way for the teacher and children to get to know one another as they first form as a class. Often we carry with us expectations of what others are like and it is important for us to get to know our class for ourselves and not to rely on others' judgements at this early stage. Group work is one way of building relationships in a public forum but let us not forget the value of the informal chats with children, perhaps as they come in in the morning or when saying goodbye at the end of the day. For the child with EBD, who may often feel left out or unable to cope, having someone take an interest in him or her as a person with hobbies, worries and ambitions can be a useful starting point. Some children seek out an adult's attention whilst others may struggle to make contact. In these cases it is important that the teacher makes the initial efforts at bridging the gap rather than expecting the child to do so. For some very withdrawn children it is far too great a jump for the child to make these connections in a large-group situation. Very often we start off with lots of partner work where we ask children to discuss a topic with another child so that they have a chance to develop and voice their ideas before being invited to share them in the large class group. This can be a useful bridge to the whole-group situation. The technique of talking in pairs is very useful at the start of a school year to giving children permission and a structure to have positive contact with a partner with whom they may not otherwise have interacted.

All groups go through this initial stage which we have already referred to as 'forming'.

Forming

When a group first comes together to carry out a task. It may range from complete strangers coming together for the first time, or a group who are familiar with each other but are starting a new task together. What they have in common is that they are to become a group for this purpose. At this stage we don't know whether they will become a group which is merely so in name only, or one which will work well together. What is likely, however, is that there will be a lot of anxiety – since those coming together are not sure of what will be asked of them, and how they will be treated. At this point the group is very dependent on the leader because it wants to know where the boundaries are, and what behaviours are permissible.

This is a familiar time for teachers at the start of the year. Although they are in the leadership position, most teachers are also feeling anxious. They are asking themselves whether they will get on with these children, what standards and rules to impose this year and so on. The children often seem subdued and watching.

It is important to remember that a new child makes the class a new group that will form and subsequently work out its norms all over again. Sometimes the impact of this is forgotten by teachers. At times teachers may blame the new child who may be struggling to establish a fully fledged identity within the class and school. When this is combined with challenging behaviour, schools may avoid ownership and treat the child as if he or she were an outsider and not a fully paid-up member of the community. The other children may also need support and understanding, otherwise they are likely to blame the child rather than seeing him or her as someone who is scared or needing support. Teachers certainly have a role to play in supporting the social contexts of the new class group and enabling other children to support the new child. The number of challenging children that move schools, for whatever reason, is disproportionately high. Sometimes the challenges thrown out are because of the move. Schools therefore need to address the attitudes and structures around including the new kid on the block.

A key aspect of group work revolves around the choice to participate. It is certainly true that you can't force someone to join in or they may sabotage the experience for everyone else. The choice to 'pass' whilst a group shares its ideas allows children to engage with the thinking without having to disclose an idea until they feel safe. We don't know what is going on in the mind of a child who has chosen to 'pass' but we can frame it positively in public by saying to the child at the end of the activity 'Thank you for listening so well during the activity'. This is an example of the use of a technique known as 'reframing', which we saw in chapter 2, and in which we suggest a way in which a child can legitimately take part in an activity. Children can be encouraged to reflect and share feelings, which can help the child to gain an insight into what his or her own feelings are. Children who state that speaking to the class feels really scary at first help others to know they are not alone or abnormal. A teacher who suggests to a child, who has chosen to opt out of a trust activity, that he/she can watch the others to see what the activity is like may enable the child to join in later. It is important to remember that what seems simple to us may not be for someone else. Trying to break down the task can aid the child to get going. Perhaps the difficulty with an activity revolves around whom they will work with. Initially, giving the child a choice will help him or her to take part in the activity.

Building up good communication, honesty and trust is our first priority and group-work exercises offer an excellent opportunity to practise skills and to raise awareness of what goes on in a class group as they get together and establish the 'how it is going to be-ness'.

With a simple listening game with clear instructions and boundaries of time and content it is not just we who can observe who gives eye-contact, who 'hears' what a child is saying, who interrupts and takes a turn for him- or herself when it is his/her partner's turn to talk – questions like:

'Who felt their partner listened really well to what they said and was able to tell the circle just what it was?'
'Can you say how you knew they were really listening?'

These questions can elicit from the group some really key points by breaking down the skills into manageable chunks.

'My partner looked at me.'
'Mine didn't fidget.'
'Mine nodded and looked interested.'
'Mine checked out at the end what I had said.'

The accurate naming of skills in front of the group is the first step to empowering children to take matters into their own hands. Just telling children to 'Listen!' is often not explicit enough. If you do listen well and know how to do it, be aware that it is not natural to everyone. Listening has to be analysed and practised as a skill.

There are many listening exercises in such books as that by Gillian Feest (1992) but for us it is the feedback from the children which is important. The 'How did it feel when you were listened to?' and 'How did you feel when someone ignored you or interrupted?' will begin to establish how this group is going to find ways forward together.

From listening exercises, we suggest moving on to activities where children who are more aware of each other can start to think about other children's needs and points of view. Again there are books to consult for further ideas (e.g. Thacker, 1990). We will give just one example here where, sitting in a circle, one child goes across to guide a blindfolded partner from his own seat, around the inside space and over to another seat, without rushing or knocking him. Care is obviously needed to ensure safety at all times. Asking the blindfolded child how it felt and why, can express for many just what a difficult thing it is to put your trust in someone else – 'I didn't like it because I thought I was going to trip over'; 'I didn't know if my leader child would sit me down on the chair properly'; 'I felt as if my partner was going to keep me safe'. Probing just that bit deeper, we'd probably follow up that last comment and ask what it was that the leader actually did to make the child feel safe. If the group is enabled, little by little, to voice, raise awareness and explore boundaries in the safety of the group-work circle, our experience is that the group starts to shift some of those things into their curriculum learning. If you started to work like this you might hear a child saying: 'I don't like it when we learn something new in maths because I think I won't get it right'; or, 'I need to know how to spell every word I use because I don't feel safe writing'; or, 'I can't do this and I won't take the risk of trying'. The messages that travel in all directions across the group-work circle mirror such statements and thoughts. We think it is possible for children to test out safety boundaries for themselves in group work before they try to do so in other areas. The child who is allowed to watch several blindfolded partners successfully complete a trust walk might feel able to pick a trustworthy child to lead her blindfolded from one area to another and say at the end of it that she was surprised and pleased at how she managed it, and that, once she got started, it wasn't the frightening experience that she imagined it would be. We've seen similar shifts in perception in children returning from outward-bound courses but, without the luxury of regular challenges like that, group-work experiences can mirror such personal growth inside school. The physical nature of many of the exercises helps to express, say, 'gentleness' in a concrete manner rather than just on a theoretical level, and thus the shift in perception stands a better chance of being generalised to playground behaviour.

As the teacher grows more familiar with the group and sees the children taking more care of one another, he/she might consider a trust walk outside the safety of the circle, which would signal the children taking on more responsibility for themselves and others. This will be an act of trust on the teacher's part as she/he will wonder: How will they cope out of my sight if their partner does not take care of them and think what they need as they are led blindfolded around the school? Have I tested out the boundaries with them sufficiently to feel that I can let go and trust the process? We think the teacher needs to tell them all this when the group reassembles. The teacher is their facilitator, but he/she is also a paid-up member of this group and has to show honesty if he/she is expecting honesty; to show risk-taking if he/she is prepared to encourage it in them. As a teacher sits in the circle along with others, waiting for several pairs of children to return with a range of responses, the teacher might feel excited, anxious, hopeful and exhilarated, and he/she will try to explain to them why, when he/she takes a turn in feeding back to the whole group. Some of the children may have had negative experiences and the teacher tells them that he/she respects what each child says in feedback. The teacher has to model acceptance of how things are, so it seems quite reasonable to let them know that you, the teacher, expect them to respect your positive and negative feelings too.

During the same exercise different children can find ways of working together so they are not always working with the same friends. This can be scary but the now familiar format of group-work exercises and activities, such as trust walks, can be repeated with different people. Such an approach can allow wonderful statements such as 'I didn't know it was going to be so much fun with X' or 'I didn't know Y was so clever'. Occasionally children will voice negative statements but by this stage they are a rarity. These can be positive learning situations where feelings can be explored and what was actually difficult – 'Y pushed me' – pinpointed so that behaviour is examined rather than just expressed as 'I don't like Y'. For both children and adults the use of 'I' statements for example, 'When you lead me too fast, I stumble and I'm afraid I'll fall and get hurt' – and the labelling of behaviour, not the child, is a useful approach to develop (see, for example, Gordon, 1974, ch. 5). The child can state to their partner what they would have liked to happen, and perhaps another attempt at the activity will give them the chance to resolve things. It is a good idea to consult with the school's Health and Safety Policy, or the headteacher, before attempting this activity.

Norming

The second stage, 'norming', comes about as the group begins to work out how it will behave. These behaviours become the 'norm' for that group. Each group will form its own set of norms or rules, although there will, of course, be similarities between groups from year to year.

We suggest that the teacher always takes part in these sessions as it is important that you listen to children and them to you. We feel that the teacher is a resource, not only in terms of experience, but also for modelling listening and sharing his/her feelings on things. There may be times when you might say 'I am sorry but I can't cope with that noise while I'm taking the register. How could you help me?'

Children sometimes offer negatively phrased solutions to problems. For example the negative 'Don't shout out in class' could be more positively expressed as 'Put up your hand to show you want to speak'. Such a change may seem minor when the intention behind the statements is similar but to tell children what to do is always more effective than telling them only what they may not do. It is also helpful for the rules to be fairly simple and observable. 'Look at someone when they are speaking to you' is easier to follow than just being told to listen.

After agreeing the positive rules and perhaps displaying them visually, possibly with photographs or illustrations, it is time to turn attention to rewards and ways to encourage children to value positive behaviour. A range of rewards is desirable because one that works for some children may not work with others. Rewards must be attainable since it is vital that the children can succeed if we are to encourage them by positive means: Children often pay more attention to sanctions or punishments, so teachers need to be alert to reinforce positive behaviour. However, sanctions are also necessary on occasion and it is helpful to have decided appropriate ones beforehand or we will find ourselves falling into the 'you're grounded for the next ten years syndrome'. Sanctions, like rewards, need to be followed through. Whilst a hierarchy of sanctions and rewards is useful, they need to be differentiated for different children. Teachers do not struggle so much with the idea that some very bright children may need different work from someone with moderate learning difficulties but it is easy to fall into the trap of seeing all children as the same when it comes to behaviour and insisting that they fit in. In some ways wanting everyone to fit in is a good aim, with which few would argue, but some children may not be ready to manage what the majority can already do. Sitting on the carpet for just ten minutes may need a reward for some children while we might simply take it for granted for most children. Boundaries could therefore be seen as elastic with children being allowed to work from where they are, sometimes being allowed to push against boundaries and learn from the experience, but always being gently pulled back until they are a part of the group and are achieving in line with the group's expectations.

It can be easy to become focused on a particular group of children within your class and to be ready to make an adult intervention in order to help those children to take positive steps. This important awareness needs to be used with discretion and sometimes children should be allowed to manage their own behaviour and resolve things themselves. The temptation to respond 'I could just sort this out quickly' may deny the opportunity for children to learn for themselves. We stress the importance of preventative rather than reactive work, like noticing good behaviour and rewarding this rather than responding only to undesirable behaviour. Avoid responding to the child who calls out and thus give him/her attention, but rather pay attention to the child sitting nearby with their hand up. This values what is expected rather than the demands of the attention-needing child. This strategy will not always work but it fosters a more positive classroom ethos.

Following work on expectations and establishing boundaries children will be keen to push against these limits to establish how safe the group is, checking out what will happen if. . . . We have called this stage storming.

Storming

In this stage each member of the group is trying to make it comfortable for him- or herself. This will bring up a wide variety of divergent ideas and values, and bringing these into an effective whole may seem impossible, particularly as individuals will display reactions learned in their best-known groups – their family or even their previous class. At the same time the group will be struggling to find its own feet, and (just as with the adolescent at an individual level) this means testing authority. After the former dependency stage this can feel particularly difficult to those in leadership roles.

As teachers we can tend to see this stage as our fault, and one of the ways this model is helpful is in bringing out the realisation that all healthy groups need to go through this stage in order to work well together. Thus storming is a good sign, not a bad one. It is not something to be avoided, glossed over, or smoothed away by the teacher, nor should the teacher be panicked into becoming more authoritarian. Rather we need to continue to notice the positives that will still be happening.

This stage of group development has no set period of time, some groups may have finished this during the first term whilst others can never fully resolve it. At times during the year, even as children move on to perform and later adjourn, then the group may go through mini-cycles of storming, relating to particular issues that exist within the class. There may even be an element of 'mourning' for last year's class that is remembered fondly from its performing stage compared with this stage of being raw recruits together.

From storming to performing

Routines and structures are mechanisms for helping all children to cope with life in school. That is not to say that there is never spontaneity, or that structure implies boring rigid lessons, but a sense of what is going on helps all to work better as a class.

It ought to be possible to have a strong but elastic structure within class that will allow children to storm and test out boundaries without damaging themselves or others. Having explored and assured themselves that this is a safe and stimulating environment, they are free to be creative and to set themselves high standards. In this environment personal mistakes and misjudgements are not harshly judged; rather there is a real opportunity for the individual to find his own solutions or resolutions and to ask the group for support. Analysing where you have gone wrong in a maths task can enable you to really understand what the process is – mistakes are informative. If you have worked hard to trace the root of your mistake, you will never forget how to do it differently. Learning can be exhilarating. Getting a tick at the end of a piece of work is, for many children, a sign that it is complete and has received the stamp of approval from the teacher. That this is just a ritual is evident when child after child fails to read the comment you have written to help them beside the tick. At times, teachers can mark to communicate with parents or headteachers or Ofsted inspectors, but just what is it they can communicate? Giving ownership of the problem back to the child can often promote higher standards. 'What else do you think you need to do?'; 'If you were to do this again, how could you do it differently?'; 'If you were the teacher what helpful comment would you make?'; 'Is there anything else you could add to this?' Given that time is short, child-to-child conferencing or conferencing in a small group can not only work for improvement but target-set for real quality.

The help of the teacher to break down targets into achievable and observable steps can sometimes be very useful for the children to maintain their enthusiasm. The curriculum can be so crammed that children never take stock or reflect on what they've done, how they've done it and what could they improve if they were to do it again. The importance of children evaluating their own work is essential if we are to build up independence. A good way to encourage this is for the adult, for example, when handed a piece of work, to adopt the role of the child and hand it back to that child saying, 'What would you say to me if I gave *you* this work? You are the teacher now. What is good? What can you improve?' The teacher can initially link work and behaviour by praising the way the children sat quietly and concentrated, or worked co-operatively as a group, and then produced some really interesting ideas. Such an approach takes time and obviously needs to be carefully managed. When children engage more in their work and recognise their successes, motivation increases.

Records of achievement are often rushed and mean little to the child. Children may choose pieces of work that are safe, for example, a piece of copied writing chosen simply because it's neat. By encouraging children to think of criteria for evaluating their work, they learn that the real values in choosing a piece of work might include 'my ideas were original' or 'I worked with somebody different' rather than simply presentation. The process of recording in their records of achievement should ideally be ongoing and serves to illustrate to children a process of thinking about work in detail and depth. The same approach can work well for some children when examining their behaviour. Children need to know what their behavioural targets are. Many children will have useful ideas about what they want to change and how they can do it. They are helped to monitor their own progress, with the teacher valuing the positive and helping them to learn from the negative.

The use of success criteria is an interesting way of developing children's involvement in evaluation of their work. This process is not suitable for every piece of work but it develops ownership and quality through a very focused approach. The school grounds committee invited a class of one of the authors to design an indoor pond in a courtyard area. During a group-work session before starting the work, the teacher and class talked about what a good design would include. Once a set of criteria was found and agreed, one child used a word processor to produce a copy for every child. The drafting began; ideas were shared, redrafted if necessary, and further ideas shared with a partner before producing a good-quality copy. These designs were then assessed by the children using the success criteria. Each child gave a score out of ten for each item in the set of criteria e.g. presentation, original ideas, use of colour, etc. Not one child asked the teacher what he thought of their design although he valued each piece of work. The children seemed to have realised when their work was good or complete.

Some curriculum areas are attractive to the majority of children. In others it is less obvious how to involve children in their learning. For example, teaching spelling may be done in a dedicated lesson, only for some children to fail to apply the skills later. For these children the use of partner and group-work techniques can be useful. Asking children, in groups, to think of homonyms can be a much more enjoyable way for children to look for words. They feel so much more rewarded when they have generated a list of words, checked them using a dictionary with adult support where necessary, than when they have been given some words that fit a pattern to copy down after a class discussion where they may have spoken once only.

Building up routines and class ways of doing things helps to develop structure and a sense of class ownership. Routine is a starting point to work from. It is at this point that the group will be in the stage of what we have called performing.

Performing

Recognising that the class group is at the performing stage of its development can be difficult at first, since as teachers we are generally geared up to noting and responding to difficulties and needs, rather than standing back and enjoying achievements. Our ability to pre-empt crises, diffuse conflicts and supply human and material resources, marks us out as members of a rapid-response team, and we seldom allow ourselves the luxury of enjoying the feeling of a well-functioning class group.

When everyone is busy and everything is running smoothly, tasks are being achieved and the curriculum successfully covered, the group can be said to be performing. Routines and boundaries have been established, children have absorbed the ethos we have set out to establish and the group has developed strategies and skills. The teacher has successfully differentiated the tasks to cater for individual needs and there is a feeling of well-being. Everything has come together, and anything is possible. This stage can be reached at almost any point in the life of the class group, and can last for almost any amount of time.

Just as group-work sessions can enable a class to explore and find solutions to problems, and help individual children recognise their own problems and find ways to solve them, so too can sessions analyse and celebrate the achievements of the class. When a class is working well academically and socially, it is tempting to go with the flow and not rock the boat by drawing attention to the fact. After all, it won't be long before something will happen to set someone off and we will have to react to the situation and start working towards equilibrium again. Why tempt fate? Let us enjoy it while it lasts!

But children can be helped to notice what it is that they are doing, and, in truth, they are doing a great deal to maintain this period of status quo and performance. The child with EBD may have become a fully paid-up member of the group by not exhibiting challenging behaviour because he/she feels comfortable with the group. This is reciprocated by the group feeling comfortable with him/her and with every other member of the group. There are still big differences between individuals but the group has reached its 'norm' and is putting its combined energies into performance.

> 'What is this group doing well?
> How do we do it?
> What sorts of things show that we know how to do something?
> How would a visitor notice?
> What do we do when there is a disagreement?
> Who decides what happens when?
> Why have we decided to do *x*?
> When will we do *x*?'

Although we don't all agree on *x* how is it that we still manage to take action?

Let us celebrate our achievements with positive statements during a group work session. Part of our growth as an inclusive group is about performing well together and we are developing a history as a group. We have had our struggles, we have had our resolutions, and now we are really up and running.

Adjourning

Preparing children for change, whether minor like packing-up time, or major like the end of year, is vital. Some aspects of routine or departure from it can lead to a class history: 'every Thursday we used to . . .'; 'that special day when we . . .'. These memorable events help to bring together a group identity and act as markers for whole periods of time or even a year. Residential experiences or school trips are good examples of this. Occasionally negative experiences viewed from a historical perspective become funny recollections and perhaps highlight the progress of certain children. It is sometimes a temptation to avoid looking at changes such as endings and let them just happen. However, by working as a group, strategies and feelings can be shared so that children do not feel alone. This is seen in the final stage of group work that we have called 'adjourning'.

Schools need to take care of the many issues that occur around transition. There is, in most classes, a yearly event as the child leaves one teacher, and possibly peer group, to join another. This is part of the regular cycle of group dynamics which begins as groups form and ends with them adjourning. Schools can support children at these difficult times through their structures and awareness. For some individuals there may be previous experiences around loss, or for others with very low self-esteem changes may be challenging. Such changes may be particularly amplified when a child changes school. In these situations group work may be used to enable children to realise that it is normal to feel worried and these fears can be explored and supported. Children can be enabled to look at issues more readily by making the worries less personal – for instance by using a worry-box for ideas that the group can explore, or by asking the class what young children would be worried about if they were to change school or class. The use of a worry-chair in the middle of the circle with another empty chair opposite can also work well when children are familiar with the technique. A child can choose to sit in the middle and offer their worry to the group. The class listens and anyone with a solution can put up his hand. The child in the middle can choose a number of solutions until he or she feels more able to manage. Interestingly, we find this approach more useful for the manner in which problems can be named and peers prompted to support each other than, necessarily, in the quality of the solutions.

This final stage, 'adjourning', is, as the name suggests, the phase when the group comes to an end. Without this phase being undertaken satisfactorily, the experience will seem unfinished and feel awkward in some way.

Groups need to look back over their time together and forward to the next step. There is often a great reluctance to part, and this may be expressed in plans to meet again.

Endings are particularly hard for some people and these difficult feelings may be shown through behaviour that seems to push apart the group.

Similarly, work levels may either increase, in an attempt to make up for lost time, or decrease because it does not seem worth bothering any more. This can be a difficult stage for teachers to deal with well given their own life experiences.

One of the things we can learn from this model is why some groups get labelled as 'difficult'. This would appear to be because they have got stuck at one of the earlier stages and cannot pass on to the productivity stage. If this is understood, and the problem identified, then it is possible to help a group overcome such difficulties.

The authors of this book believe that the work we are advocating is appropriate for all children. It is important that if, as we believe, we should work towards social inclusion, we begin that work now and do not wait for a really challenging child. How can we truly include everyone in our classrooms? Inclusion isn't about making everyone the same but about equality of opportunity to join or not. We recognise the spectrum of emotional and behavioural needs that arise in and out of school and every child can be seen to have gifts and special needs. If we are to include challenging children then what better place for teachers to begin than in their classes! Setting up an inclusive community within the class certainly helps to value individuals and what each one has to offer. Having stated this, there are often children in a class or adults in a school who find it difficult to fit into a system, for a wide variety of reasons, and these individuals and systems may need support. This group is not static; individuals may become included over time in the class whilst others may find their role changes. We can all think of times when we have felt left out or not a part of things. The teacher can be aware of the children in their class who may be temporarily, or in the long term, excluded from joining in. Simple strategies, such as checking people are not left alone and are working together effectively, can help get things going. The following two case studies illustrate how the same teacher manages two very different situations at different times with different classes. The first is more generally about inclusion in her classroom and the second recognises the very specific challenge of working with a class to support an individual child.

Odd one out

Sometimes you get children in your class who get left out socially; they're the last to be picked for a side in PE; the last to be chosen in partner work; the ones nobody wants to sit next to; the ones you often see on their own in the playground. It worries me. In fact, it worries me more when I think about it. They can be ostracised from the group for a whole variety of reasons and they can handle their 'status' in the group in an equally wide variety of ways, ranging from provoking and hitting out, to suffering in silence and never making their needs known. They all share a common fact that the group cannot accept them and they do not know how to make a difference for themselves.

Think for a moment about how it might feel for a boy (or a girl) to be the odd one out. If he tries to give of his best in the classroom, absorbing new information and responding to questions, achieving his own personal success, he is likely to alienate the group even more. If he is praised by the teacher in front of peers who don't accept him it will marginalise him further, even more because the group do not want him to do well. If he remains quiet, in a world of his own, not listening but perhaps thinking how he is going to survive the next playtime, he may get picked out by the teacher for not concentrating, and then get taunted in the playground for being stupid or thick. If he stands out in class and acts out some of his problems he is more than likely to lose the sympathy of the group who resent his attention-seeking. If he is left out in collaborative work in class, he can be dealt a double blow: peers who turn their back on him, and a teacher who incites him to 'hurry up and find a partner' so that she can start the task.

He cannot win. He is not liked. He doesn't much like himself with the weight of the peer group against him.

I haven't got any children with extreme needs in my class this year for the first time ever but I can pinpoint three children who are not really accepted by the group.

Diana drifts in and out of relationships and can hold a sulk at the oddest of times, and friends tire of her unpredictability. She is quiet and reserved and has what the group considers to be an irritating habit of gravitating towards any adult who visits the class. She seems to crave adult attention and will monopolise and play up to men and women alike. Diana is always left to last in team games, and friends often forget about her at lunchtime because she is holding the dinner lady's hand, chatting animatedly about this and that.

Susan has something about her that other children don't like but, try as I may, I can't spot what it is. It seems to have come with her up the school and is long established. I do notice that she does not stand up for herself or stop friends when they take advantage of her generosity, but she is an OK child with nothing obvious about her. Several years back her single mother had a struggle managing herself in the neighbourhood, and Susan developed an old head on her shoulders looking out for her mum. Things have sorted themselves out for the family but Susan remains with the same peer group and I can imagine that history has remained with her.

Sean arrives at school without a jumper, coat or lunch box some days, and finds it as hard as his mum does to remember information and to organise himself and his belongings. He is quite a drain on the natural generosity of others. He always needs to borrow a pen or PE kit and often does not recognise his own lunch box at home time. He can sometimes hurt other children or take small objects from under their eyes but he is quiet and fairly 'innocent' in the way he is.

Susan is an able child, Diana is of average ability and Sean is of lower ability. This group is, however, uncomfortable for them and I think it would be valuable to change that.

In group work I chose to do a leadership game where I take the first turn leading the class in a sequence of physical actions. We are all seated in a circle. First, I clap rhythmically and the children join in. Then I pat my knees, and within three or four seconds everyone has noticed and has followed suit. I change to shaking my wrists and clicking my fingers. The level of listening and watching is good and I transfer control to a confident child in the circle. She is a respected 'leader' in the group and they quickly switch allegiance and follow the lead. When Diana assumes the role of leader she is tentative at first – it's new territory for her – but she responds to being given the group's approval and carries out an excellent set of moves – innovative ones which are later copied by another child in the leadership role. At the end of the game we have a round of statements: 'How did it feel?' Diana's comments are interesting: 'I didn't know how to do it at the start because I didn't think anybody would follow me, but I found I could do it after a bit.' Mary picks up on Diana's comments when it's her turn: 'I wished I'd had a go, but there wasn't time, was there?

Can I say something about Diana? I thought she did some really good moves for us. I think she was thinking about the rest of us.'

Having a Mary in the class is a godsend. She is perceptive and articulate and is respected in the group for being able to give feedback about just how it is. As it is generally not my practice to comment on children's statements in these rounds, I leave it to the group to think as long as they need to before the next child decides to break the pause with his or her statement. The gap speaks volumes – is it perhaps a signal that we might think a little differently about Diana? It's a sort of intuition that the group develops if I let them. Only a few seconds but I choose not to fill it with my adult 'making-sense-of-things' voice.

I notice one thing about Diana that week. She is invited to be a team leader and to pick a team in netball. She doesn't get to choose more than a couple of children because she was prompted and urged by the others to pick whom they wanted, but she has been allowed a different role and she did play more decisively in the game.

Next time we had group work we worked with large sheets of paper and fat felt-tip pens, breaking up into small groups to brainstorm, in pictures and captions, 'times when I feel left out, at home and at school', 'how I feel when I'm left out'. I put them in groups of four with each of the key children in a different group.

When we came back to the main circle, and each group shared the drawings and captions, there were surprisingly clear similarities, however the children had chosen to represent their ideas.

Even perceived leaders with high status in this group had very strong experiences to share. When I asked what we had heard from one another, three or four children voiced their surprise at discovering 'We are all the same – even the teacher!' I had joined a struggling group and they had described for me my own feeling of being left out.

This felt both vulnerable and bonding – part of our shared history as a group. We moved on to another round of statements: 'When you feel left out, what do you need for yourself?' These were the statements:

'I need a friend to notice.'
'I need to walk away from it.'
'I need to go and find some other friends.'
'I need to tell the dinner lady.'

'I need my mum.'
'I need to thump them.'
'I need to get out my toy and hope someone will come and play with me.'
'I need someone to tell me what to do.'
'I don't need anything.'
'I need to think in my head and decide what to do.'

Almost everyone gave a reply. Everything was heard and not adjusted or made sensible. We moved into the same small groups to brainstorm ideas for, 'When I feel left out these are the things I could do'.

Sean, Diana and Susan were more animated in their groups this time. It was not their sole problem any more, and they could see this now. I hoped that by pooling ideas each child in the class would have access to strategies they couldn't have thought of on their own.

After the feedback, Annie brought a problem to the circle. 'When I want to play with my friend sometimes she won't play and goes off with the dinner lady. Then she comes back and says I won't play with her, and the dinner lady says it's my fault.'

Yes, it's Diana. The left-out child who manages to get herself left out by her own actions and then feels hurt and rejected when she decides to join in again.

Up till now, we'd been aware only of Diana's feelings. The level of trust and perceived safety in the group seems able to allow such risk-taking on Annie's part. We'd be less than honest not to tackle this real plea here.

'Annie, how do you feel when this friend goes off with the adults? Can you say, because your friend may not have realised that it bothered you?'

'I feel sad and left out, and cross.'

'What would you like to say to her?'

'I don't like it when you go off. I want you to stay with me and play!'

'Have you ever tried saying that. Maybe you could because it might be helpful?'

I ask the group for ideas on this problem and there are some great suggestions for Annie to choose from and for the un-named Diana to hear.

'When the girl goes off she might need to, but I think she could promise to come back later and meet by the climbing frame.'

'I don't think it is fair to go off with adults when someone wants to play.'

I check with Annie that it is OK to leave the subject and close the session with a round of: 'Next time I feel left out I'm going to . . .'

On reflection, I can see that not only have we explored the common problem of feeling left out and how to deal with changing things for ourselves, but also the underlying issue that we have some part to play and can own our own behaviour rather than assuming it is someone else's fault. This is not a cosy exercise – it is not a game in a circle – it's about finding out together what it is like to be in a group. For me as a 'proper adult', I'm prepared to show them that I can learn too, and I'm going to talk to someone at the next gathering I find myself in instead of waiting to be noticed!

I've always worked on the premise of trying to get it right for everyone by giving them access to a common language with which to express their differences – a sort of arbitration process. I don't believe that Sean, Susan and Diana's 'left-outness' is far removed from Miles's and Rikki's (children with statements of special need associated with EBD) inability to get on with their group. It's all on a spectrum of behaviour and intensity. For Diana to own her own part in putting people off she has to go through the same process as Rikki owning that he provokes and winds others up when he is feeling threatened and on his own, and therefore gets shunned by potential friends.

Diana was left to ponder on Annie's disappointment whenever she chose to spend the lunch hours with the dinner lady, and the class was left to reflect on Diana's latent ability as a leader. They will have made sense of their experiences, moved on and changed some things for themselves without further adult intervention. And what of Susan and Sean now they have focused on feeling left out? Things will have moved on for them too. They seem to have gained from discovering that everyone feels left out at times, and that there are several strategies to use when they feel themselves in that situation. They, along with the rest of the class, have heard from the teacher that they are valued members of the group and that the group ethos is to accept differences and to find a place for all, even when there are difficult issues to be faced.

Some of the ideas sown then will have germinated, others will have been forgotten, a few will have been nudged and nurtured in the context of the classroom. Children will have talked amongst themselves and decided which ideas are important and useful to

> them in their day-to-day interactions. The peer group will have some of the tools to support and understand individual members, and individuals will have had personal access to their teacher to further explore issues that affect them.

In this scenario it has been so much more than the teacher talking to the class and encouraging them to include the odd ones out. Everyone has been involved in the process and there has been real endeavour to maintain the initiative within the peer group.

Including Miles

In this final section we will give extracts from another case study where we see one of the authors reflecting on her use of group work at three points in the integration of a child with EBD. In the first section we see her in a planned session, before the child started in the class, helping the group prepare for the arrival of Miles. The next section similarly describes a session at which Miles wasn't present, where the teacher helps the class make sense of their first impressions of Miles. The third extract shows how the group tackled the introduction of a special programme for Miles.

Preparing the way

Miles joined our class in February, six months into the school year. I had not met him but had snippets of information about him. He had autistic tendencies, was partially sighted, had a palsied hand and leg and was intellectually gifted.

If I expected the children to accept a child at the extreme end of the behaviour spectrum, then I needed to have them involved every step of the way, and they needed language with which to make sense of things.

The first session, which was without Miles, gave me the opportunity to give a potted case history of his physical disabilities, touching briefly on the idea of 'autism', but really dealing with how it might feel to have little stable sight. Miles had very little sight and in only one eye, and his focus flickered, making reading tiring and giving him a fairly narrow field of vision.

We often did trust-walk exercises (see Thacker and Feest, 1991) treating our blindfolded partner to positive experiences in the classroom and in the wider environment of the school grounds. On this occasion, partners encouraged their blindfolded partners to write down their names; to choose coloured cubes from a pile; to cut out a circle from card and to find their book folder and PE kit in the crowded classroom.

With our eyes back to full strength, we tried tying shoelaces with one hand only; then doing up zips and buttons single-handed. It was a great leveller.

Reflecting on the exercise, the statements ranged:

> 'I felt really frightened when I couldn't see.'
> 'I got cross with myself.'
> 'I thought it was OK.'
> 'Pass.'
> 'I didn't like it – not being able to do easy things.'
> 'It was like being a toddler again.'
> 'It was lonely'.

By raising awareness I hoped that they would not all rush up to Miles and grab his arm to lead him around or start speaking loudly to him.

Miles arrives

Miles made sure this didn't happen. He didn't like children near him at that stage, and, being highly articulate, he told them just how independent he was! He loved delivering speeches and could answer questions like a politician. He was not yet able to allow anyone else the luxury of uninterrupted speech, and would complain and huff and puff loudly when anyone else was speaking. He was acutely jealous if I, as his teacher, listened to another child or gave praise. He protested often that he hated children and that nobody ever listened to him or said a good word about him.

After a couple of weeks Miles was spending more time in class with us; there were new adults around working to support him, and the feeling of novelty was wearing off. Tensions were building up in the group and children who were trying to accommodate and support him were receiving flack and verbal abuse from him. He was meeting more and more situations that challenged his autistic tendencies, and children and adults were getting physically hurt by him.

Over the weeks when Miles was settling into the class, group-work sessions were on demand whenever anyone in the group needed to off-load, ask for information or share good points. These sessions could be set up for just a few minutes or for half an hour whilst we discussed strategies or reinforced how we wanted it to be for Miles and ourselves in the group. Sometimes we just met for celebration and reflection.

First impressions

We set up a group-work session while Miles was out of class and tried to make some sense of what was happening and what we were noticing about ourselves. Looking back it was a really significant meeting for me too. 'Is there anything you noticed that you didn't like or understand?' was the prompt.

I shared with them that there were things that were worrying me; there were things I was pleased with; things that bewildered me and things that amused me. As usual I was real and honest. I had been delighted when Miles and Billy had enjoyed a game of pirates together. I was amazed that Miles made such a good effort to read out his story with expression. I was cross that he kept interrupting me when I was talking to another child about something special.

Well, the floodgates opened and a picture of huge complexity emerged. There were jealousies, there were fears, and there were genuine triumphs and celebrations. As we shared in the circle there were connections drawn between some of Miles's behaviour and the tantrums that younger brothers and sisters had. So we steered ourselves to a round of our own worst toddler anecdotes. Somehow bringing his behaviour in line with our own put a more human face on things. Each of us was still capable of 'throwing a wobbly'. It was just we hardly ever did it, whereas Miles did it all the time.

When we saw Miles in this framework, things became amusing rather than frightening, and I was surprised to hear all the positive suggestions about how to manage alongside an irritable toddler. The session finished with the prompt, 'Now that I've talked, I feel . . .' and 'I'm going to try *x* when *y* happens'. I chose not to tell Miles the details of our group-work sessions this time because he had very little perception of how he affected others at that time. I did, however, feed back some of the positive comments about how well he was doing. There had been many of these.

Slogging along

This was a time of hard work for the group but they kept at it, and core members continued to offer encouragement and positive statements to those of us who were flagging in energy and enthusiasm. I was at quite a low ebb too.

It was also hard to start reflecting things back to Miles about his behaviour. If you offered him a compliment he questioned it. If you offered him a bit of advice or marked a maths problem wrong he flew into a rage about it. If you praised another child he intervened and started grumbling and destroying the child's self-esteem before your eyes. If anyone showed thoughtfulness to me, he immediately questioned my acceptance of him and made a substantial fuss.

I was struggling emotionally, and Linda and Kathy, who shared classroom assistant duties supporting Miles, were receiving verbal abuse and some physical treatment at his hands.

We were working on a system of rewards and sanctions but these weren't effective, I think, because he had not responded to a similar approach at his previous school and had brought some anxiety with him about such an approach. Quite clearly he did not understand what was required of him and did not even seem to be aware of a 'happy face' or a 'sad face' in the adults around him. Children were even more removed from him. He claimed to dislike them all and I did not see him take any personal interest in them.

A new idea

Dave came up with a different idea. As SENCo and nurture-group teacher he experienced Miles in a smaller group of very needy children, but with a group which had a highly developed vocabulary in group-work terms. One morning he stated his intention to try and physically hold Miles through and out of the other side of his next temper tantrum. And so he did – exhibiting a wonderfully gentle firmness and a measure of belief in this difficult and distressed little boy. Mum said that this had never been tried before but she was immensely supportive of all efforts made for Miles and was gaining in her confidence in his ability to continue in mainstream education.

I told the class about this approach and explained that I would like to do the same thing when Miles exploded in class. We worked out what they needed to do to keep safe and what I needed to do to manage physically. We didn't have to wait for long for plan A to be needed and they sprang into action. They moved tables to one side, removing chairs and themselves from the site of the tantrum and bringing me a chair to sit on whilst I contained him on my lap. Because his glasses often got hurled across the room, somebody held them for him and I was aware of a sort of space around us, and some very respectful watchers.

He did not bite himself as he usually did and as the anger subsided, he ended up seeming to enjoy the physical contact that had turned into a hug. Now that his shouting and ranting had subsided I started to praise and encourage him and have a conversation about what he would like to do next.

Later on, we were given some old PE mats and a number of sofa cushions to set up a soft corner in the room for temper tantrums. Other children used it in their own way and benefited tremendously. It was also a flopping-out place. Then, later, it became the only place the entire class would gather to talk about current affairs and newspaper reports!

In the longer run

These early tantrums were long and angry but were manageable. No longer did Miles tip over chairs or push children round when he flew into a rage and only once did he direct any anger towards me, threatening to bite me but checking himself at the last moment.

Tantrums lessened very quickly, and by referring to them when he was at ease with himself, Miles began to build up a vocabulary and a history of 'when *x* happened I was able to do *y*'. He improved fast and worked hard, learning to reflect not only on the feelings that led to his tantrums, but also on the effect he had on the others.

First of all he recognised when children were happy for him or pleased by what he did, admiring his drawing, his reading or his writing. Later he could 'hear' but not accept negative feelings. It was a huge struggle to acknowledge cause and effect.

Children in the class were accustomed to looking at each other and saying, 'I don't like it when you do *x* to me' or 'I like it when . . .' and they offered him the same treatment. Little by little he took an interest in them, and I can remember the day he gave a compliment to a child face to face for the first time.

Concluding comments

As a way of summarising the teaching principles underlying this work we are reproducing a series of statements based on a grounded theory of educational principles with illustrative comments from teachers. These are drawn from tables 1–10 in the previously mentioned book about Fernhill School (Thacker, 1998, pp. 368–77). These principles represent part of the grounded theory that emerged from the first cycle of our work at this school when we looked at the educational theory and practice used by all the teachers. These principles underpin the present work of the second and third authors, which is illustrated in the case studies throughout this book.

Grounded theory statements of educational principles with quotations (in italics) from interviews with teachers

Summary I

All are learners on an ever-changing journey undertaken as a community. A common process of learning is encouraged involving: think, make decision, plan, take action, review, reflect, learn. Children are fully involved in this proces. Teaching is about facilitating this process for children.

Statements I

Both teachers and children are seen as learners on a journey.

> *I make every effort to facilitate learning and to model learning to the children.*

Educational opportunities are provided, both in the classroom and in the general life of the school, which allow the children to take part, reflect on the experience and then to extract their own learning from the activity in cooperation with their fellow pupils and the teacher.

> *I believe that children can plan, negotiate, reflect and review, given the right support and encouragement and I value what they offer.*

This is seen as a life-long process of learning and relearning which involves both adults and children. The school is seen as an organisation where all are learning.

> *I am not complacent about my own or anyone else's knowledge. Having celebrated what each person has, I am always looking for ways to coax new targets to work towards.*

The children are involved in much of the decision-making. There is an effort to provide opportunities for children to take responsibility in ways which they might not otherwise have. Giving responsibility is seen as part of the real respect for individuals shown here.

> *I believe that even the youngest child can be helped to recognise who and where he is, and to move forward to where he wants to go. Every child has within him the capacity to explore his own potential to the full, and to achieve it.*

Summary 2

Space and time are given to all to allow thoughtful reflection and creative action.

Statements 2

The teachers' experience of being given space and trust inclines them to give the children the same sense of space and trust in their own class teaching.

This space and trust are seen to benefit the children, who respond creatively to educational challenges even if it is necessary for them to struggle and keep trying.

Time and space to think is seen as important. Children are allowed to think in their heads before making a response.

> *I will hold boundaries of time and space for the group but within those boundaries there is always time and sufficient space for each child to explore and investigate.*

Silence is seen as allowing a person to concentrate on his or her own inner thoughts. This is seen to help produce creative ideas.

This sense of space and time to be heard may contrast with 'busy-ness' in some homes.

Summary 3

Teachers trust children to give of their best. In such conditions of trust these people strive together for excellence in fellowship and not competition.

Statements 3

Work of real quality is encouraged. The staff have high standards for their own work and the children are encouraged to find their own standards. This is done by not praising or blaming the child for the work but directing them to their own sense of quality.

> *I trust children to know themselves and their capabilities and I will help them to know themselves as members of a group.*

The pupils are encouraged to set their own standards and strive to raise them, helping one another to achieve the best outcome for all rather than competing against one amother.

> *I feel that children are capable of taking responsibility and growing towards independence.*

> *Academic excellence is not the only achievement to be celebrated, and I give equal weight to anything that is genuine personal achievement.*

> *Self-competitiveness seems far more healthy than competing child against child and succeeding on someone else's failure and humiliation.*

Summary 4

Risks are taken as part of a creative struggle. Support is always offered and failure is seen as instructive and not to be condemned.

Statements 4

It is recognised that to achieve this sometimes involves a risk of things not turning out as expected but this is also seen as an opportunity for learning. There is a freedom from criticism and a supportive atmosphere. This is seen as a spur to creativity.

> *Negatives and mistakes are often the best stimuli for learning and I try to use these positively. Analysing why you have gone wrong in a maths task will allow you to really understand what the process is, and, having worked hard at it, you will never forget how to do it.*

> *Personal mistakes or misjudgements are not harshly judged by me, but I try to give a real chance for the individual to find his own solution or resolution and to own the consequences of his action.*

The children are encouraged to be independent and to find their own way to solve problems. They are allowed to exercise initiative without needing to ask permission all the time.

> *I give permission within the group to try to do things differently and to develop initiative. When something is 'going wrong' in the group, there will be an expectation that it is everybody's responsibility to sort it out. All are expected to struggle to find a way forward, adults and children alike, and the adults do not come out with rules or cut-and-dried answers. The resulting solution is thus 'owned' by everybody.*

> *I think learning can be exhilarating, risky and rewarding.*

Summary 5

Child-centred education is valued more than imposed, didactic teaching of a prescribed curriculum. This child-centred approach is seen to achieve high conventional standards.

Statements 5

There is an emphasis on practical, inquiry-based, first-hand educational opportunities, undertaken in a cooperative fashion and in a supportive classroom environment.

> *However, I do not expect children to re-invent the wheel, and investigation and exploration also need clear models and tried-and-tested examples alongside them.*
>
> *I believe it is possible to have a strong structure or framework which allows creativity and originality to flourish. Boundaries do not have to be limiting – they can allow freedom and growth within them.*

> *I believe that each child has a right to grow and learn in a supportive, stimulating and challenging environment.*

However, it is understood that some children and parents hold a view which might be expressed as 'They can't be working if it is fun'.

Summary 6

Teachers and pupils are encouraged to be present as real people, not just in role. This involves accepting the less attractive sides of people and life and struggling with difficult issues, not avoiding them.

Statements 6

Adults consciously see themselves as role models, and how they are with each other and with the children is seen as a lesson. Thus they recognise a need to work on themselves as adults as part of the educational offering made to children.

> *I am me, with the children and will show my own disappointment, irritation, humour and stillness. At the same time I will always be aware that this is a group that I am responsible for, and I am the boundary keeper and will help at the interface with dinner ladies, parents, other staff, visitors, the community, etc.*

> *I dislike 'games-play' and I do not play games with the children. I expect children to be real whatever that involves and will offer safety and support.*

'Realness' is prized. The teacher makes real personal connection with the children. They do not stand in role. This is seen as a risk since being open and friendly is often connected to not being respected. In this framework, however, the respect is seen to grow even more rather than being diminished.

But being real also means having to acknowledge and accept the less attractive sides of people.

Education is seen as part of the real life of the children, not just as a preparation for the future.

Summary 7

Group work is seen as an important teaching process, consciously undertaken to develop self-knowledge through cooperation and involvement with others.

Statements 7

Group work is central to this approach and can be applied right across the curriculum.

This is not seen as a set of technical exercises but as a way of encouraging a genuinely cooperative approach to learning.

It is seen to be about personal transformation and accessing each other's humanity. Development is from the inside into self-awareness. It is a personally engaging, experiential approach.

The head and the heart need to be in harmony, but it is seen that we may need to support the heart in our overly cognitive tradition. Children may need a chance to express their feelings.

Diversity and differences are celebrated as well as things which can be acknowledged as common to all.

> *I think differences can add so much, and whether they be within the child or between home and school they need to be welcomed into the group and woven into the learning experience.*

People are seen as whole beings and physical contact and closeness are also part of the tradition. This can lead to easy natural relationships between children and adults and children.

Summary 8

All people are given respect and are listened to carefully.

Statements 8

Good listening is seen as important in giving everybody the respect that is their due. Teachers take children seriously and listened to them.

> *The children are encouraged and trained, through group work, to listen to each other and hear each individual viewpoint.*

> *I respect children and encourage them to respect me and each other.*

Summary 9

The way adults interact is seen as directly affecting the way adults deal with children.

Statements 9

There is an awareness that the way in which the leadership role is exercised affects the way in which the teachers interact and this, in its turn, affects the way the children are treated.

Chapter 4

A supportive school is a resilient school

The previous two chapters have considered the personal processes of teachers and the context of the classroom to explore ways of supporting children with the EBD label. In chapter 2 we saw how the attitudes of the teacher make a crucial difference as to whether or not children with EBD are accepted in a class. In chapter 3, we saw how teachers can build a supportive classroom using groupwork principles and mobilise other children to help with their inclusion. These are certainly good starting points for teachers as they have great influence over them. In a recent article Richards (1999) states: 'Indeed, there is some evidence that successful adult support cultures exist and function successfully even where the staff's general attitude to the management's support role is negative' (p. 102).

However, it is to be hoped that a school can do something better than this, and this chapter looks at the wider picture of the whole school and recognises that the classroom is not an island isolated from the rest of the school community, even when it is situated in a portakabin some distance from the main building. We will show what elements go to make a supportive whole-school community, in particular by the leadership and the organisational culture which is created. Individual teachers not only make a difference to the children they teach but to the schools within which they work. Similarly, the school has an impact on the teacher and the class. There is an echoing between the class and the school. This chapter explores ways in which teachers can be supported by good leadership and, in their turn, how they can help the school to operate a successful policy of inclusion.

Reynolds and Sullivan (1981) studied eight comprehensive schools in Wales and found the more effective schools to be characterised by an ethos of 'incorporation' and the least effective schools displayed an ethos of 'coercion'. This 'coercion' ethos held negative attitudes towards pupils, seeing them as being in need of containment, control and character training. They employed deficiency and deprivation explanations for the high level of behavioural difficulties they observed in their pupils. Teaching and management strategies tended towards the confrontational and punitive, and staff–pupil relationships were impersonal.

The 'incorporative view' was characterised by teachers who had a positive view of pupils and their parents, a recognition of the essential worth and individuality of each child, and a commitment to the aim of eliciting the voluntary involvement of the pupils and parents in school life. Teaching and management styles stressed pupil responsibility, self-discipline, and involvement. Staff–pupil relations tended to an interpersonal style, not an impersonal one, with stress on mutual respect and partnership. Learning and behaviour problems tended to be approached in a therapeutic manner with the emphasis being on the pupils' need for support.

In a recent study, Richards (1999) confirms these findings from the point of view of students identifying the factors that characterise an inclusive school. He reports that the most significant factor is that adult behaviour should be 'supportive, non-judgmental and non-threatening' (p. 100). He also identifies a need for adults 'who have the time and motivation to listen to their problems and take action with and for them if required' (p. 100). He also reports that in successful inclusive schools adults are keen to adopt a pastoral role and are easily able to merge this with their subject-teaching function, by using subject content as a tool for addressing personal and emotional development as well as using pastoral issues to place subject-teaching content in context.

Whole-school approaches and developing consistent practice through a school is something that has been regularly encouraged over the past ten years in many areas of schooling ranging from areas of the curriculum to behaviour. The necessity for a whole-school behaviour policy that can promote consistency and a team approach to working with challenging children is therefore not surprising. However, such a document is meaningless unless consultation and involvement of various school groups, including parents and the wider community, has taken place. For the authors of this book such a policy is a framework that supports and reflects practice. It is not about setting up rigid frameworks that stop flexibility and creativity of response. Revision of the whole-school policy provides a regular opportunity to reflect and consider the way behaviour affects the school and the process of learning. Having thought about strategies in advance means teachers don't have to think from scratch on their feet. As Richards (1999) found, an inclusive school curriculum content is examined to supply 'meaningful and relevant knowledge and skills at a level that provides challenge and achievement' (p. 100). Accreditation is sought which best motivates the pupil rather than what achieves the best league-table statistics and an emphasis is placed 'on avoiding problems through motivating and stimulating lessons rather than on systems for controlling behaviour'. Records are carefully kept which avoid the use of emotive language so that parents can be properly communicated with on a regular basis and proper information can be sent on to other schools when it is necessary for the child to move on in the system.

As we have already seen, it is adult attitudes that are at the heart of good inclusive school practice. Richards reports that in such successful schools:

> Adults avoid perceptions of inappropriate behaviour as a personal threat to their own status or power and examine these external signs for indications of cause . . . [They] adopt problem-solving approaches to emotional and behavioural difficulties and seek solutions to causes and avoidance of triggers rather than suppression of symptoms.
>
> (1999, p. 100)

Points to reflect on

In our school:

How do we recognise individual worth?
In what ways do we involve parents?
How do we encourage self-discipline and motivation?
What do we need to do to achieve consistency in our whole-school response to children with EBD?
In what ways are the pupils given responsibility?

Why do schools maintain such different attitudes? Looked at from a systemic point of view, one can speculate that teachers who behave coercively will find evidence to support their actions and beliefs in the responses of the pupils and staff. In the same way teachers who behave in incorporative ways will be doing so with the background support of an incorporative school culture. The prevailing ethos has a big effect on new teachers and they are inducted into the culture that exists. Thus it may be that an act of faith is required and that a headteacher can have an incorporative vision for their school which, when achieved, creates a positive interaction between staff and students, and this feedback strengthens the vision still further and new staff are inducted into this positive experience. Perhaps we are dealing with a self-fulfilling-prophecy effect here with negative, coercive schools producing 'evidence' in the children's behaviour to support their approach? If this is so, then perhaps we need leaders of vision to follow an incorporative view and they will gain similar 'evidence' but this time this will consist of a positive response on the children's part.

The importance of leadership and organisational culture

The importance of leadership and organisational culture has been the experience of the authors of this present book based on their involvement in a research project which, as we have already seen, carried out a two-year study of leadership and organisational culture in an English primary school (Thacker, 1998). In this study the whole staff, including the headteacher, were fully involved in the research using a model of cooperative inquiry (see, e.g. Heron, 1996). We have already seen the detailed statements of the educational principles which form the grounded theory which emerged in this study in chapter 3. In a similar fashion we will end this present chapter with the grounded theory which emerged to describe the leadership and organisational culture of the school supported by interview quotations from the headteacher. We do this on the basis that both the teacher authors of this book, Dave Strudwick and Elly Babbedge, were members of this culture and were influenced by the leadership of the school.

The school had a particular emphasis on pupils with EBD and at one point the school was noted for taking in a number of children who had been excluded from their previous schools. All of these children had statements of special educational need and the money which was allocated to meet their needs was used creatively in this school in a number of ways including the formation of a 'support group' which was run by Dave Strudwick who also acted as Special

Educational Needs Coordinator or SENCo. At the end of this chapter the case study will show what is possible when a school uses resources in this way and in the context of the leadership and organisational culture described in this chapter.

The significance of a systemic approach

There is a growing awareness in many schools that the complex problems that occur in education may need complex solutions. A systemic approach to working with children with EBD allows the school opportunities to see things differently and avoid blaming. A systemic approach views emotional and behavioural problems as having to always be considered in context since they are often a response to the particular context of family, peer group or school. Attention is paid to the particular way that the person concerned sees a situation or is, in turn, viewed by other people involved in the situation. 'This relates to other aspects of the environment, such as rule structures, patterns of organisation and routine which influence the social climate of a situation and might be described by the term "ethos"' (Cooper, 1999a, p. 7).

Systemic thinking may allow us to recognise the importance of school structures such as the length of the lunchtime alongside the individual child's difficulties in making friends. As such, every member of the school community may have some way of building the solution. It is not the sole responsibility of child or classteacher but the collective responsibility of the school. How can the peer group give support? What can a parent offer? It also allows seemingly unrelated areas to be joined together. The school organisation, where MTAs (meal-time assistants) are isolated in their role, may produce poor behaviour at lunchtimes with particular children acting aggressively towards the MTAs. Systemic thinking stops us from going straight to the child to rectify the problem but helps us to ask the important question: What can I do in my role? Perhaps addressing another piece of the jigsaw will resolve the problem? In the given example, one part of the intervention may involve raising the status and support of MTAs or training them in running lunchtime activities or in improved teacher–MTA liaison. Such thinking allows us to search for solutions and promotes the belief that there is not one set response or course of action to the problem, but many.

We think that when you hear the statement from schools that 'we've done everything possible and now it's up to the child' it is very likely that things are set up to fail. That is not to say that such work is easy but solutions can always be created if the vision and the will is there.

Assemblies may have more potential than many schools realise. They are not only opportunities for being together and building a school's culture but are reflections of the way that a school functions and includes people. Even if this does not directly make an impact on the child with EBD, then it gives a sense of the context for him/her. This is best done by giving positive messages at assembly times such as praise for good work and achievement.

Staff meetings highlight the way school functions and these processes cascade outwards towards the children. If staff cannot listen to one another, why should a teacher be surprised when the children cannot manage to do the same? Examples of the importance of assemblies and staff meetings in reflecting and enhancing an organisational culture are contained in the study by Thacker (1998).

Transition times such as children moving up to another class or arriving from another school or changing from primary to secondary phases of education need to be planned for. Schools should be aware that as these changes provide new contexts, and the child's behaviour may well be different now, a fresh start can be given. Previous schools need to consider any label they may be passing on whilst being honest in their opinions. Just managing to hold on to a child and then hoping 'that things will be OK' in the next school is not the same as identifying areas of progress that the child made or difficulties that occurred. It is unfair to lay the blame for the high exclusion rates around the transition to secondary from primary schools solely at the door of the secondary school. Secondary schools and their feeder schools should look together at their procedures for transferring children.

A wide range of issues affects the way in which schools manage the children who challenge them. A school's ethos or culture is unique and, although when schools say 'we do that' when referring to a particular issue or process, they may carry it out in a very different way, which reflects the characteristics of the members that make up the community. Even something as apparently uniform as SATs may be tackled in a wide range of ways. Whereas in some schools they are strongly promoted and the pupils coached in the necessary facts for the entire term and a half in order for the school to be seen in a good light politically, in another school they may be seen as an opportunity for staff to give children an opportunity to check on their learning as well as to prepare for the tests.

At times, cultures use certain groups as scapegoats and it is helpful for schools to be aware of this. As we have already seen, usually people are chosen who have little formal power, such as the child with EBD and his or her parents. It could be that these children are a symptom and not a cause of a system dysfunction with the result that blame is regularly transferred to a certain population. It is important for teachers to question their own culture and beliefs. Probably we have all heard the labels that go with particular individuals, both adults and children, in staff room conversations. That is not to say that people shouldn't offload or say what they are finding difficult, but simply that it is possible to do this without blaming. There is a huge gulf between the statements 'I'm finding Wayne challenging' and 'Wayne's a pain in the neck'. The first helps people to know you may need some support whilst the latter possibly builds fear or at least the expectation that Wayne will be a problem. We should not be surprised, then, when the person fulfils the expectations, with increasing effectiveness, as the label begins to stick. Schools may have expectations of certain groups that are too high or too low. Being able to critically review ourselves, or honestly listen to outsiders, can help move schools on in this area. For this to happen, it is essential that members of the community are heard, taken seriously and, although there may not be agreement, they need not be blamed.

The strength and support that can come from working with others inside and outside the school can be vital. This could be someone with whom to talk through ideas. Support can be available through the head, the school SENCo, a friendly colleague, or someone from another school or an outside agency, such as an educational psychologist. The key is for teachers to find someone who listens to them, without judging them, and helps them to find a way forward. The availability of SENCos allows opportunities to work collaboratively and to get into teachers' classrooms so that they can value what the teacher is doing, talk with him or her about what needs to happen and jointly work towards some solutions. Such work gives opportunities for new learning that can be experienced in a real context allowing all to move forward. Through working with an outside agency, the teacher can gain new information and skills, as well as the confidence to make changes in his or her practice, and even to support others with their teaching.

Helping the individual child

There are many structures that may be set up to allow adults and children, including the challenging child, to manage the school day more easily. A quiet area outside for lunchtimes, a school council that gets children involved in the running of the school, or a school counsellor with whom children can talk through worries, may all contribute to a flexible response. It is worth noting that these interventions can be seen from several different perspectives. For example, the child who gets extracted for a group that supports social skills may enjoy the activities and the opportunities for working in a smaller group, but may also be aware of the label that comes from belonging to such a group. It is tempting for us as adults to recognise the progress that children make and the adult endeavour behind them as purely a good thing when in fact it may also have a negative element for that child within the whole school, and we must work to reframe this positively.

Creative support

Funding is an important issue in making provision for the child with EBD. Unfortunately many schools take a linear view that the child who is difficult can be 'sorted out' as soon as funding is found to provide one-to-one support. It is tempting to slip into the 'just managing' role while reports are prepared and meetings are convened. If we adopt this holding position, however, we can miss out on discovering valuable strategies which can build up working relationships with the child and with the peer group he is learning to operate in. Extra funding can push on strategies and relationships, but it cannot often produce a magic cure.

The statementing process takes time and we need to be creative in the meanwhile not only with our ideas, but also with our existing budget and the deployment of staff. Can the SENCo take the class for an hour and release the teacher to stand back and observe dynamics in the classroom? Could the teacher shadow the child with EBD using a running-record sheet focusing on the child's interactions, listening skills, independent strategies, etc.? Is there an opportunity for the classteacher to be released for a short time to problem solve with a child, share a skill, have fun with the child?

Supportive colleagues don't just have to give you ideas for coping with children, they can also use their people skills to give you confidence in your own abilities.

When funding is found there are choices as to how it is used to support the child with EBD or children. If it is used to appoint a learning support assistant (LSA) we need to ask ourselves how we are prepared to give that adult support in the classroom and in the school community. We also need to think about the type of support we expect the child to receive in such a relationship. We suggest that, more often than not, the child needs to be moving forwards and developing strategies for independence, relying less and less upon the LSA. At a very simple level, the two following interactions illustrate points on a metaphorical scale of adult support.

Child: What have I got to do?
LSA: Don't worry. I'll explain it to you.
Child: What have I got to do?
LSA: Look, the teacher's free at the moment. Why don't you go over and ask her what it is that you need to do. I'll help you with it when you get started.

Tuned into the child, a good LSA can sense when it is time to push on for a bit more independence, and when it is more appropriate to consolidate confidence and play safe. Facilitating a relationship between teacher and child in a busy classroom is beneficial to both parties. We include some examples of prompts used by one LSA on her journey with a child with EBD.

> 'I'm going to watch you work for three minutes to see how many things you can manage to do on your own.'
>
> 'I could count how many times you put your hand up to answer the teacher.'
>
> 'Let's see if I can notice you using your word book in the way we usually do.'

Now a shift of ownership to the child:

> 'You put a block in the bag every time you put up your hand to give an answer.'

'You mark down on your tally-chart each time you look up when someone says your name.'

'You turn over the sand-timer and see if you can write for three minutes.'

At a later stage in the journey:

'What target are you going to set today?

'How are you going to measure your success?

'How will you know when you've reached the target?

'Do you need to give yourself a reward this time? What will it be?'

Notice the move from 'I, the adult, will do this for you', to 'you, the child, keeping track of what we are working on'. The final challenges invite the child to make choices, practise independent strategies and evaluate success.

Funding can be used in a variety of ways to support a child. The following section outlines some of the possibilities that arise from working with a child who has funding for full-time help from a learning support assistant, and the benefits that arise from connections with outside agencies. The approach shows that not only the child but also the rest of the class/group benefited from such work.

Flexible help

Paul came from a Psychiatric Assessment centre after being excluded from his previous school. He was very streetwise and some of his challenging behaviour came from his frustration with a specific learning difficulty relating to writing. It was a challenge to arrange support in ways that this very bright Year Five child could access without having a babysitter with him. At times this was best done with the support assistant being around in the room or working with his group. The support assistant was used for both an individualised programme and for supporting access to class activities. There was a balance to be sought. The SENCo also released the classteacher for one lesson a week to do an individual project with the child on the computer. This was something he enjoyed and helped to build a firmer relationship with the teacher after a rocky start. He had some one-to-one support from the school caretaker with whom he had made a strong relationship. For this situation, the caretaker, although not trained, provided the school with an opportunity and proved to be the best person to support the child with his reading, writing and maths within the class and with one-to-one work. The support/training for the caretaker followed from a recognition that he was a key person rather than trying to find someone with appropriate training, hoping that they would be right for Paul. It also gave the child a chance to help the caretaker with some practical tasks around the school. Paul loved the opportunity and initially this was a great reward for good work.

As time developed and the relationship grew, the caretaker linked well with the parents and supported the child to face up to the difficulties of writing and recording his excellent ideas. After a few terms, we reviewed the child's progress and decided to reduce the level of support by a day. This sent a great message to all concerned that the child was doing well and was developing independence. It was not about reducing things too quickly, but allowing the positives to be nurtured and for us as adults to not start clucking that 'this child won't manage' or 'what if something happens and there is no support?' If something did happen, as it did with other non-statemented children or children labelled as severely EBD, then we would manage as best we could. We also received support from a psychiatric nurse, who made a half-termly visit over the first year after the child had started at the school. This was useful for me as it provided a different perspective and person with whom I could sound out ideas. It was also good for the child who could have his progress acknowledged by someone else he valued. This support was also available via phone when needed. Similarly we had regular contact with the therapist assigned to Paul by the hospital, who was interested in his progress in school. Paul was also given a laptop after an IT assessment. Initially he used this a great deal but later he decided he preferred to write. The parents were also fully involved and regularly came into the school and worked hard to support their child's learning at home. He gained from the SENCo getting him books of a lower reading age but an older interest level. Paul came to the nurture group for three afternoons a week to help him develop the social skills to manage more easily in groups such as his class group which he had initially found very threatening. In all, a multifaceted approach was used to support this child. It met the needs of the child and those of the context in which we were all working. This was certainly a success story up until the child left the school at the end of Year Six.

Building relationships

As we saw in chapter 3 the importance of relationships is as important in many respects as the narrowly prescribed academic curriculum. A wider curriculum should look, not just at what we learn, but at the processes of learning and also include learning about ourselves, our emotions, about each other and the world we live in. Schools must find ways to avoid seeing the child as only a behaviour problem and to lose track of the learning that is their entitlement. The authors of this book recognise that this learning is likely to be of a social, emotional and academic nature, with each complementing the other rather than each being exclusive.

As we have stressed above, what seems most important, for any of a number of strategies or processes to work, is the quality of relationships between members of the school community. Some teachers may find themselves isolated from other staff within their school but they can still make significant differences to their class and, gradually, to the system. It may not be easy in some schools to be the advocate for the challenging child; in fact it can be hard not to be drawn into a cycle of negative expectation. An isolated teacher can still find ways forward by staying focused on his or her class and finding an ally with whom to talk. Quite often other members of staff may feel similarly but find that it is impossible to say anything. Gradually, if teachers can find support from other colleagues within the school, they may find it easier to say what they really mean and act correspondingly. In some situations, finding a colleague from another school may be helpful. The school's efforts to get it right for these challenging children are as important as the outcomes. These children, who often feel that nobody likes them, may consciously or unconsciously pick up the intention behind the actions. The value of schools, who want to get it right for these children, should not be underestimated.

The following case study allows us an opportunity to explore in more detail how a particular school culture used funding from a number of statemented children previously excluded from their original schools. Various forms of adult support were combined with a classteacher's perseverance and skill to work together with parents to support a very needy and demanding child.

In an honest admission Rikki's classteacher, Elly, recognises that she never really hit it off with this child and that he in his turn found it particularly hard to relate to females, including female teachers. Despite this,

> I think I did a lot of practical things to help him, and I acknowledge that he had some happy times with me. But, believing as he did, that he was the reason behind everybody else's problems, I was never able to convince him that he was OK for who he was. It's a two-way process when you come to build up a relationship with a child and I was forever building bridges out into the river and hoping that he would start out to meet me. For a very long time Rikki stood on his distant bank and threw missiles to try to sabotage my construction.

Back when he joined the school in Year 2 in another class:

> For three or four weeks he got into fights, interrupted with smart comments, silly replies and irritating noises and moved around the place at speed, taking things to pieces and never settling. He was talked about in the staff room with a wry humour that told everything about how exhausting he was in a class. He was the type of butterfly child with tons of physical energy and loads of questions. He challenged everybody and everything and showed aggression and irritability.
>
> He found it difficult to make friends and each playtime resulted in complaints about his actions, and with children in tears or well and truly wound-up. He was exhaustingly vocal and as a thought popped into his head, he voiced it. He had developed a loud and penetrating line in whining and complaining.

When he joined Elly's class, which contained thirty-six Year 3 and 4 children, they went on a trip to the museum.

> After a lively coach journey he reached the museum and became a whirling dervish, beside himself with nerves, excitement and devilishness, lacking any sort of self-control whatsoever. He and I missed the rest of the trip and remained in the entrance hall waiting for the others to finish their learning. I watched him and talked to him, containing him when I really had to but also grappling with my own understanding of his behaviour. At first I thought that if I

saw him as a child of three years old, then I would understand, but what was coming across was that, whatever stage of development he was at, he was a very distressed child totally uneasy with who he was.

What I had done by taking him to the museum was to take him away from any safe boundaries he had at school or home. Open-ended tasks brought out the worst in him and here at the museum everything was uncertain and he had no props but me.

In class he alienated himself from all the children except Matthew who was rapidly becoming his victim and needed a bit of protection. Rikki was able to voice that everywhere was the same – everyone hated him – and this had been the same at his old school. His brother hated him and his mum and dad hated him and they were divorced because of him and the way he was. I also hated him, didn't I? Significantly, he stayed still to listen to me, although he didn't give any voluntary eye contact. I said that I liked him a lot. I talked about his behaviour being something different and this was, or seemed to be, well out of his comprehension then.

That Rikki was an angry boy was not in question, but his anger was very hard to defuse. He was so angry with himself that he regularly cut, tore or screwed up his work or drawings and declared them not good enough. I could not convince him that I felt something was good or that another child thought something was good. He was un-persuadable.

He had a particular gift for design and drawing and was very observant. It was something of a retreat for him to sit and draw when everything else was too difficult, but in the early days he did not allow much to survive. He would be sketching quietly in a corner, far away from anyone else, when he would explode into anger and destroy his drawing, complaining bitterly about himself. His drawings were never done in his sketchbook, which remained unused, because he seemed to think they would no longer be his and would belong to school.

This attitude, now I come to record it, perhaps said more than I realised at the time. I remember feeling slightly irritated that he would not use the book or accept my reasoning that he would have a collection of drawings to keep at the end of it.

In the back of my mind, of course, niggling away was my teacher accountability. If anyone asked what Rikki had done what would there be to show?

Support from a colleague

Let us now hear from Dave, the other teacher involved in this case study, who was then the teacher of the support group. This is a small flexible group which the school had established with extra help provided by the SEN statements of a good number of children in the school. He observed:

> The sense I had of Elly's class, on the few brief occasions I was in there, was of crowdedness and of a teacher with amazing child-centredneess. Some of the children in her class, however, seemed to be finding this approach threatening or difficult. This group of children was quite sizeable, certainly six. Elly often referred to how Rikki affected the dynamics of the group, and left things feeling tense and fraught. However, although it felt as though Rikki was really making it difficult for Elly, her language was different from that of some teachers. It was not blaming and showed a genuine concern to make it all right for Rikki in her class.

Eventually, there came a point when Elly needed help and the flexibility of having a small nurture group proved of worth.

> One day in November, ten weeks into term, I got to school and I just couldn't face another struggle with the group. I had no energy left; I had lost my humour; I had lost my ability to tolerate his constant 'in your faceness'; I had lost it in every way. I felt so tired and sabotaged that I believed I might not be able to be fair to Rikki that day and I know that the rest of the class were showing similar feelings and were beginning to turn against him. It felt out of control and unhealthy and I had to break into the situation to reform and recharge in order to help Rikki.
>
> What we did felt like the only option I had left and I believe that it was right to do it. Dave, who already had Rikki for a few sessions when his nurture group were doing PE or art, volunteered to receive him full-time to give me some respite, and to work with Rikki when he came back into my class. The importance of having a colleague to support me in this way was huge. It was an emergency action; we hadn't planned it, so I hadn't had a chance to talk to Rikki's mum or dad about the change, albeit a temporary one.

The importance of reflection

This was obviously not ideal and Dave reflects on this.

> In hindsight this was another mistake. It would have been beneficial for me to have met the parents at an earlier stage to present the positives of what we were going to try to achieve. Luckily, though, we recovered from this mistake. Although Rikki's dad was understandably concerned and a bit aggressive at first, he soon calmed down and was quite emotional about his concerns for Rikki. Mum and dad were both concerned about their son missing out on work but soon realised from what we were saying that he was bright and that until he learnt to manage the social side of school, his learning, in an academic sense, would never take off. Rikki was not at this meeting but we fed back a potted version afterwards.

Finding a way forward together

> Rikki's initial experiences in the support group were quite varied. I certainly assumed too much in his case. Rikki, as a Year 3 child, seemed quite a lot younger than the others who ranged from Year 5 to Year 7. This made it quite difficult for him to relate to some of the children and vice versa. However, one of the positives came from some of the older children trying to take care of this younger child. At times the group, particularly early on, needed reminding that this boy was younger. He did not present with a great deal of difficult behaviour at this time. I did not have the feelings that others stated that this boy brought out for them, except that he really needed to be cared for. Rikki's biggest challenge to me and the group at this early stage was his calling out when others were talking during group-work sessions. This appeared to be not deliberate but resulted from a lack of awareness of how we were working. Gradually he began to hold his ideas longer and wait for his turn.
>
> Rikki was now annoyed at not being in his class and desperately wanted to be there. We chatted on a number of occasions about what had been difficult for him and how he could change some of the things that had happened. I tried to suggest concrete strategies and specific examples rather than saying, 'When you go back in your class, you must improve your behaviour'.

> During more academic sessions, I noticed how Rikki's low self-esteem initiated poor behaviour in some work contexts. He was worried about getting things wrong, particularly spellings. It was hard for him to accept that when I said not to worry about the spellings that I meant it. Once he did get going, he produced some very creative stories. He was relaxed when he was drawing and he enjoyed illustrating any language work he had done. Rikki was keen to read although he again lacked confidence. Some of the books in the support group therefore really suited him as they seemed for older readers but were actually of a lower reading age.
>
> He was keen to share his work with Elly, which was very positive. It felt like one of those situations when two people didn't realise how much was already in place. Elly's efforts were not in vain. However, because of the stage things had got to it was difficult for Rikki to return. I thought it must have been difficult for Elly to deal with not being able to manage. It is one of those ridiculous expectations that many teachers put on themselves, myself included, that 'I must always be in control and things must always be seen to be good by others'. If Elly was feeling these things, I felt she would need a great deal of support to manage Rikki in what was a demanding class.
>
> We began to integrate Rikki back into his class in small doses. He was not able to cope with twenty minutes so we dropped it to five, and built up from there. Once Rikki achieved some success, he quickly began to build up his time in class. Eventually he was in class for about a third of his week. He had been very much involved in what was going on: being asked how he thought he was doing (he found this very difficult); getting feedback, and being involved in joint target-setting. The targets during this stage were kept simple and focused mainly around calling out.

This extract from Rikki's case study shows plainly the effectiveness of colleague support in enabling a classteacher to return to a situation that had temporarily exhausted and confused her. Her advocacy of the child had not been dampened despite a personal challenge that had led her to ask for help. Time to reflect and to recharge enabled her to take up the challenge again. The flexibility of the system in which she found herself meant that there was practical support on offer too, and a custom-made package of experiences was worked out for all concerned, including the parents. The adults all shared the attitude that the child is central – something which is at the heart of good inclusive school practice. Rikki altered the package over time as he took increasing responsibility for himself, and again, the system allowed for this. Although inherently flexible, this school's system had not been used in such a way before but lent itself readily to new demands. Individual teachers not only make a difference to the children they teach but also to the schools within which they work. The classroom is not an island, particularly when it is part of a resilient school.

Concluding comments

In this chapter we have seen the many benefits of maintaining a flexible and supportive approach to dealing with children with EBD. We have looked at how this has to be at a school-wide level and have shown how the organisational culture makes such flexibility possible. The role of the headteacher is crucial in creating and maintaining this culture and we will conclude the chapter by looking at the grounded theory statements of an organisational culture with quotations (in italic) from interviews with the headteacher. This is the culture in which many of the case studies in this book are located.

Summary I

All are learners on an ever-changing journey undertaken as a community.

Statements I

To be a member of the school community is like being part of an ever-changing and moving journey both individually and together. All are seen as learners continually engaged in the process of learning, reflecting and relearning on this journey.

> *I have a strong personal commitment to growth and change in my personal and professional life and have always been learning and changing within education.*

For wholesome learning to take place there is a need for an awareness of the individual self to be seen alongside an awareness of the self in the wider community.

Summary 2

Space and time are given to all to allow thoughtful reflection and creative action. Such space and time is safeguarded by leaders managing boundaries and controlling the demands made on class-teachers.

Statements 2

The staff perceive themselves to have the space and freedom to act. They feel trusted to act according to their own professional ideas.

> *My leadership style can be divided overall into leadership actions which I undertake and which might be called 'hands on' but, equally importantly, through what might be described as 'hands off' aspects of leadership. In this latter class the most important thing is that I give a psychological space where trained and committed professional teachers are trusted to help the children in their care to learn and develop.*

This gives them a sense of being able to get on with their central role as classteachers with energy and creativity.

> *I am very active in managing this boundary and I use my professional experience to monitor the demands made on the school community from the outside.*

> *I control rigorously the amount and type of demands passed on to the staff by using my vision of the nature of the school as the criterion for choice. It is this function above all others which creates the impression of space to get on with their job which, I think, is so appreciated by the teachers in this school.*

Summary 3

Trust allows self-motivated people to give of their best. In such conditions these people strive together for excellence in fellowship and not competition.

Statements 3

The effect of being given space and trust by the head is seen to encourage staff to find their own path in their work in conditions of little or no judgement but with the support of colleagues. This does not seem to lead to sloppiness but rather to high standards which are self-maintained.

The head is, however, also seen by the staff to be knowledgeable about what goes on in the school and to have high standards for himself and for others.

There is not a sense of competitiveness but rather a shared sense of striving to achieve high quality in all that is done and in a spirit of genuine cooperation.

> *My approach of trusting staff and allowing them space to get on with their job I think works with the skilled, self-motivated teachers who thrive at this school.*
>
> *This makes the choice of teachers to work in this school of particular importance as is the recruitment of self-motivated, conscientious and competent staff who share something of my vision. Thus my formal power, especially my role in selecting staff, I see as crucial in getting together a group of staff who respond with self-determined high standards.*
>
> *I see this form of selection as a two-way process. As the school has developed its particular distinctive stance, so people have been attracted to apply for posts and, once in post, have chosen to remain and play a part in developing the culture.*

Summary 4

Risks are taken as part of a creative struggle. Support is always offered and failure is seen as instructive and not to be condemned.

Statements 4

Learning is seen as dynamic and involving some element of struggle and frequently fear. An element of fear is inevitable if risks are to be taken. Without an element of risk, there is less chance of new learning being possible.

My history within the school has been of struggle and taking risks in trying to realise my vision. This is a creative search summed up by the phrase 'Anything is possible'.

A central idea here is that the constructive freedom to take risks gives energy for people to be creative. Being creative is made easier by failure being seen to be instructive and no one is judged or treated harshly for trying something which does not work out as they expected. This creates a feeling of safety in which people can extend their own range of learning experiences.

Summary 5

Child-centred education is valued more than imposed, didactic teaching of a prescribed curriculum. This child-centred approach is seen to achieve high conventional standards.

Statements 5

I have consciously tried to introduce 'child-centred' teaching methods from the time of my appointment.

I am aware that this does not find favour with some parents or recent government statements. However, I see myself as an experienced practitioner and have confidence in my own ideas which I am prepared to maintain in the face of opposition.

This 'child-centred' style is seen as being in contrast to an approach with imposed, didactic teaching of prescribed curriculum content using competition between children as a means of motivation.

It is recognised that this view of how high achievement is attained is not shared by all parents, some of whom would prefer a less trusting, more competitive approach.

However, there is a strong internal professional view that teachers can cover curriculum requirements very well using these approaches and that this can be demonstrated in conventional ways such as scores on attainment tests.

Summary 6

Teachers and pupils are encouraged to be present as real people, not just in role. This involves accepting the less attractive sides of people and life and struggling with difficult issues, not avoiding them.

Statements 6

Self-discovery and self-exploration are particularly encouraged as being essential aspects of growth for all members and there is a high priority placed on the development of the whole person.

> *All that I do is informed by the vision I hold for the school. An important part of my role is to hold to the vision even when the staff are caught up in the everyday things of a school. This allows it to be constantly rekindled in the interactions I have with the staff and pupils.*
>
> *This is not some 'vision' dreamed up to look good on some organisational mission statement but is part of my real life. I do not draw a sharp distinction between the personal and professional parts of my life, seeing them as facets of my real self. This is generally expressed in this culture as 'being real' – acting from a core sense of self and not from an idea of professional role.*
>
> *This quality of commitment is what I try to model for the staff, and I think it is echoed in the adult organisational culture.*
>
> *Indeed 'being real', being prepared to take risks and to struggle with difficult issues, are central to my image of myself within the school.*

This links in with honesty, integrity, authenticity – being 'real' – and with personal connectedness being sought, worked at and always encouraged.

There is a stress on the importance of being a real person, fully present in the community and not just according to the expectations of a role.

This is helped by the recognition that all need to recognise and acknowledge the negative or shadow aspects of themselves so that this is not projected out on to other people.

This means that people are encouraged to take responsibility for their own actions and not to be always blaming others.

It also means that people are allowed to be fully themselves and are valued not merely for their role but for themselves.

Summary 7

Group-work is seen as an important teaching process, consciously undertaken to develop self-knowledge through cooperation and involvement with others.

Statements 7

Most staff see the role of group work, especially the associated training, as a key factor in the forging of a distinctive culture.

> *I see group work as equally applicable to teachers' interactions as adults as it is to classroom practice.*

Summary 8

All people are given respect and are listened to carefully.

Statements 8

I try to ensure that I am visible around the school, and this makes me available to the staff in an easy, informal way.

This valuing of each member of the community creates a feeling of support, trust and safety. There is real respect between people and all are free to speak and are listened to carefully.

Summary 9

The way adults interact is seen as directly affecting the way adults deal with children.

Statements 9

There is an atmosphere of space and calm which is both modelled and facilitated by the leader.

> *As well as the freeing of time made possible by efficiently managing the outside demands made on the school, I see another, more symbolic action. This is the modelling of a lack of 'busyness' by making space for myself from time to time. My way of doing this is to just sit in a central and highly visible place in the*

school, perhaps having a cup of coffee. What I want people to think is: 'If it's OK for him to stop, maybe there is no need to panic or go into a frenzy'.

A real connection is established between the leadership displayed by the head and this organisational adult culture. The influences mentioned in these summaries and statements are seen to 'cascade' down in their turn to the culture which the individual classteacher creates in interaction with his or her pupils.

Chapter 5

Home–school relations

The manner in which homes and schools can work together to help children is the topic of this chapter. In the primary school it is the classteacher who spends most time with the pupils in his or her class and who is usually responsible for contacts with parents and for their personal tutoring as well as personal and social education. However, as we pointed out in chapter 3, most secondary schools are too big and specialised for the pupils to stay together in any one group. For this reason most have adopted an organisational arrangement whereby each pupil is in a group where one member of staff can get to know them well. This form of organisation and the way it is coordinated through the school is known as the pastoral-care system. In most such systems in secondary schools, each teacher will have one class for which they are responsible for the well-being of each pupil. In primary schools this is the classteacher with his or her own class.

In chapter 3 we saw how the meetings of such a class, sometimes referred to as a tutor group in secondary schools, is often the time when that part of the curriculum to do with personal and social education is taught, and we explored how group work could be a means of delivering this part of the curriculum.

However, such work is only part of the pastoral-care system of any school. Let us look at a list showing the goals of such a system:

1 to provide a point of personal contact with every student and an appropriate relationship to hear and understand their experience and their view of progress;
2 to provide a point of personal contact with parents to hear their hopes and fears for their child's progress;

3 to monitor each individual student's progress and achievement across the whole curriculum and to create an overview of his or her approach to different learning tasks;
4 to use the knowledge of students' and parents' perspectives in offering support and guidance to students on any issue which affects their development and achievement;
5 to provide colleagues with relevant knowledge of students so that their teaching efforts can be adapted for greater success;
6 to promote the development of teaching and learning and a school organisation which respond to the experiences of students;
7 to encourage a caring *and* orderly environment within which all students can exercise initiative and develop;
8 to mobilise the resources of the wider educational, welfare, community and world-of-work networks to support and extend the experiences of all students (Watkins and Thacker, 1993, p. 4).

In this chapter we look at the role of the teacher at primary level, or form tutor at secondary level, as providing a point of personal contact with every student and with his or her parents and with wider networks who might offer additional support to pupils.

Involving parents in supporting children

Let us look at positive strategies that schools can use to work collaboratively with parents in order to support their children in school. Finding ways of including parents, guardians or carers varies from school to school. Historically, parents have not always been made welcome in school. The manner in which schools relate to parents and the way the two support each other can make a big difference to the progress of the child in school through, for example, the following:

- induction programmes;
- written information from school to home to some or all parents;
- newsletters to keep parents informed of what is happening and what equipment children need, although these will not, on their own, help parents to engage with schools;
- open evenings and days to encourage parents to work with their child's school; some schools operate a weekly parent slot either to look at the last week's work or to voice any concerns;

- tutor–group evenings (in secondary schools);
- progress review meetings for individual students;
- home visits on a routine basis;
- curriculum evenings where new topics or approaches are shared with parents, who, in terms of their skills, are frequently an untapped resource; they can be asked to support specific pieces of learning where they have appropriate expertise and learning in general;
- schemes for practical support for school programmes at home, for example, follow-up activities for the reading approach used in class;
- parent/teacher social and recreational events;
- parent classes or groups to meet expressed needs, e.g. in coping with adolescent behaviour or ways of helping school entrants to settle in reception classes;
- formal representation and involvement in the management of the school; parent governors have been given increased influence thanks to recent education acts; parents can also be involved and consulted in the development of school policy; being asked, 'What works?', 'What doesn't?', 'What you would like to happen?';
- parents can link to governors, to a parent–school association or other groups; schools are often at the heart of a community and so may host a range of activities that encourage parents into the school for activities or events;
- class teachers being approachable and non-judgmental may help parents to become involved with their children's learning; teachers simply saying 'hello' to parents can be a useful start;
- since parents spend so much time with their children, their opinions should be listened to seriously and their perspective incorporated into any plans made for the child.

These last two points are well illustrated in the following case study where one teacher (Elly) explains how good relationships can be established with the parents of a challenging child.

> There is always a lot of story-telling to be done when I first meet with the parents of a challenging child, and I really value the connection we make. More often than not it has been a struggle for the family to get to this point and there is generally a lot to tell: episodes, clashes, failures, attitudes, achievements, etc. And I want to hear

it all – really sit there and hear it all. I don't want to make too many comments or ask too many leading questions. I don't want to put my interpretation on things that I'm told or offer my own solutions, and usually I have to have this first history-telling without the child. I try hard to accept whatever I hear and to remain unjudgemental, and, most important of all, I set out some boundaries of confidentiality and time:

'We have twenty minutes or so and I'd like you to tell me whatever it is that you'd like me to know about your children. I'm not going to be able to offer any quick-fix answers but I'd like to go away and think about what I have heard from you and meet again in a few day's time to see where we can go on from here.'

I believe that, as primary caregivers for this child, the parents are the experts on him. They hold more information about him than I ever can, and I trust them to select the pieces which they would like me to know as his new teacher.

I might give some feedback after the story-telling, whatever it has been. It will have been immensely helpful for me and I will want to respect the parents who have probably worked hard to entrust information and experiences to me.

It has been reassuring to see parents relax and flourish given this ownership of their child in school. They have often expressed surprise that they have not been challenged or felt judged, but have been listened to. By being listened to they have not been able to ramble on and on but have known there is a time boundary and that the child is central to the meeting. Yes, often they will be wanting to describe quite a bit about themselves and their own childhood, but the guidance is there to bring them back with prompts from me like 'And how does this affect your son?' or 'And your son?' I am there to set up a working partnership with each party feeling they have a voice and a responsibility, and that the child is absolutely central.

I might finish the first meeting with an invitation for the parents to tell me one thing their child can do well or one thing about their child that makes them proud. It can be a huge challenge for them. They might not have the vocabulary with which to do this since they are so used to telling the negatives, the conflicts, the problems. No matter if they find this impossible. It will be a bit of homework to think about and something to bring up at our next meeting, perhaps with the child's help next time.

Let us continue with our list of ways of involving parents:

- Provide opportunities for them to join shared day-time classes.
- Involving them in the everyday positive aspects of a child's development. All too often parents are contacted only when a child does something wrong. Catching a parent at the end of the day, sending a letter home, special assemblies where good work and behaviour can be valued or sending home good pieces of work or certificates are all good practices.
- Encourage them to help in the school. For some parents this involvement may give them strategies for managing their own children. Where a sizeable group of parents work in school and gain first-hand experience of working with staff, that school may find advocates who convey favourable impressions to other parents.

These points are illustrated in the following case study by Dave, which shows how providing opportunities for a parent to be involved in the classroom can provide help for the child by helping the parents. This stated, it must be acknowledged that such change usually takes time, and the personal resilience of teachers is important.

> One particular experience of working with a parent helped me to change some of the culture of blame that exists around parents. A very needy child that I worked with, who was very immature and had been abused by a person outside her family, was often coming to school dirty. Other children commented on this, and this further highlighted her isolation in the group. I regularly talked to the child's mother and whilst I tried to explain things about what her child managed as well as her difficulties in the class, I never really felt that this mother heard me or understood what I was getting at.
>
> I could get changes in concrete ways such as ensuring that Mum managed to give the child clean clothes but this seemed to be dealing with the symptoms. Mum couldn't get my picture of letting her daughter grow up and become more independent so she was not so different from her peers. (This Year 5 child was not allowed to turn on taps at home on her own.) The child wanted to be like her friends but without going against her mum's wishes.

The two experiences were so far apart that it left the child confused and unsettled. Things changed when I stopped focusing on the problems and invited Mum in to work in the class. I didn't want Mum to work with the child, as this would add to her label of being immature. My aim was for the child's mother to get a view of her child with her peers, seeing what sort of things they did and enjoyed. What I did get was a very powerful sense of this mum's love for her daughter, wanting to protect and care for this most special person. Once I appreciated this, I worked more positively with the child's mum. She worked less with her daughter and enjoyed the responsibility of working with others in the class. She gained confidence in her own abilities and began work as a mealtime assistant in another school. Once I had shifted my perception and focused on solutions, it was much easier to find positive routes forward.

The child as a link between home and school

This last case study shows the child being 'confused and unsettled' by the differences between home and school. Children play a large part in the link between home and school. As Osborne points out 'All children are part of the two overlapping systems of family and school and they usually take the strain of mediating between them and of adjusting to them both' (Dowling and Osborne, 1994, 2nd edn, p. 36). At times they may say one thing to school and another to home. A common illustration of this is the way problems can develop between home and school over the issue of homework. For some children plenty of help will be available. For others there may be none. For some children home may be inappropriate for such work because of overcrowding and having no private space in which to work. The use of homework clubs or rooms can aid this, but schools need to be aware of these issues when trying to ensure equality of opportunity. Any broad policies need to be interpreted sensitively to allow for families who find it hard to cope at any particular time.

Expectations

As mentioned in the previous chapter school systems may carry their own expectations of groups that are perceived as problematic. Sometimes teachers may stop making an effort or just expect, because they work within a difficult catchment area, that you can't do or achieve some things with 'our children'. Demographic features do have an effect but these should not be used as an excuse for not exploring other courses of action. Similarly, in apparently well-functioning groups personal and social education is equally relevant.

In a culture that often blames teachers or parents for the shortcomings of the society, it is important that schools don't pass on such blaming tactics themselves – *or* fall into the trap of labelling groups of parents or particular parents.

Taking care not to reinforce the label

At times schools can seem to collude with parents and go down the route of 'isn't this kid awful', thus getting drawn further and further into focusing on the problem as opposed to the possible solutions. When a child annoys adults at home and school, it is possible for both to be reacting to the negative behaviour with increasing amounts of punishment and similar ways of seeing the problem. When this happens they can be said to 'mirror' each other. Whilst a recognition of what is difficult is helpful, it is also important that we remain solution-based so that bridges can be built. We have all heard the parent who says their child does this and this and this, and, whilst listening to their problems may be helpful for the parent, we need to ask, at least to ourselves, 'What does the child do that is acceptable?'. Teachers, too, can reinforce a poor label by catching a parent at the end of the day in a crowded playground and letting mum or dad know what a trouble Johnny has been. This encourages Johnny's reputation to build up and he begins to fulfil the expectation that he cannot manage. Particularly in a small rural school, the strong sense of community can leave some families so labelled they become scapegoats and isolated.

When both school and home see the child as the problem, it becomes increasingly likely that a medical and pharmaceutical solution will be used. We are not against medication in every case; if it is used as a short-term measure to enable the child to change, it can be helpful. However, what we frequently see is the use of drugs for children who could manage without if they were treated differently, either at school or at home. It appears to us that, all too often, drugs are used as a band-aid for a system's problems. You cannot give a whole school a tablet for its disfunctioning! Such an approach can reinforce a child's label making change more difficult and leaving children believing they can only manage when they take their pills.

Is a change of school indicated?

School and home can get to the point where they are not communicating and everything seems to be going wrong for all concerned. For some parents in this situation, a change of school may seem the only option. Frightened parents can do the proverbial 'moonlight flit' and disappear without warning, hoping to give their child and themselves a fresh start with no historical baggage. Others can arrive at the new school and heap mountains of blame on the place they have just left. Thus the parents of some challenging children can move from school to school, never allowing difficulties to be faced and worked through. How much better for the child, parents and school if all can gain confidence and effect changes for the child in partnership together.

However, in some cases, a change of school can be beneficial. The child and his/her parents may feel that the new school will be more understanding. We have already quoted the example (see p. 20) of the headteacher who surprised and delighted the parents of a boy with EBD by saying that the child would be 'a gift to the school'. This set a positive tone for the placement, and the child, as we reported, made great strides in learning and behaviour in that school.

What is it reasonable for a teacher to do?

It is important that, while being sympathetic to children's needs, we also stay focused on what we can realistically do as a teacher. So often we hear teachers saying, 'If only he didn't stay down the park so late . . .', 'If only he didn't hang around with those boys from the estate . . .'. Such statements set us up for failure as we have little or no control over many of these things. We can help children develop social skills and the ability to make wise decisions out of school, but we cannot change their lives at home.

Some of what we can do or offer will depend as much on our skills and relationship with the child as on the particular problem. Some teachers are very adept at using counselling skills in their everyday work, allowing children to name things and hear them reflected back, for example, and then supporting the child as he or she looks for ways forward. For more details of such skills presented in ways which are suitable for regular classroom teachers, and not specialist counsellors, we would refer readers to Eric and Carol Hall's 1988 book, *Human Relations and Education*, and to that of Watkins and Thacker (1993). It is important that we should not underestimate the capacity to help that we have in our role as teachers, but conversely we need to recognise our own proper boundaries.

Dealing cooperatively with parent–teacher problems

All children with EBD will need parents and teachers to get together to sort out problems from time to time. We suggest that a three-step model drawn from Watkins and Thacker (1993, p. 186) and reproduced below with some modification is a basis for any parent–teacher problem-solving meeting.

The exploration phase

- Recognise and share perspectives. This involves an honest expression of views and careful listening to the other point of view in turns.
- Create a climate of shared concerns and goals.
- Manage time fairly.

Developing-new-understandings phase

- Work on perspectives with the aim of getting a more productive way of seeing the problem. This should lead to a new goal that incorporates the needs of all the parties.
- Make a commitment to work for a win–win solution if conflict arises.
- Use your joint imaginations to get lots of ideas about how this goal can be reached.
- Decide jointly on which of these new options you want to choose.

Action phase

- Make a plan.
- Decide whether it is practicable and sustainable and whether you value it.

- Decide who'll do what.
- Decide how you will recognise whether this has been done.
- Agree when and how it will be checked. This may include agreeing to meet again.

Coping with difficult situations

It is extremely hard to stay focused and calm when an irate or threatening parent is facing you at the classroom door because they have a concern about their child or the school. It goes against our instincts of 'fight or flight' which make us want to turn our backs on the problem or put up our fists, actually or metaphorically, to defend ourselves and maybe return a blow or two in the process. As teachers we may quite often be in the firing line and we need to learn how to handle ourselves professionally. When parents come into school ready to fight their corner for their child they may have insufficient information or even the wrong information. Parents, for a range of reasons, may feel extremely threatened and vulnerable about having to come into the school at difficult times. Which of us, when feeling like that, can put forward our best side and be rational and reasonable? In such circumstances, it is helpful if one of the parties knows something about resolving problems productively and peacefully, and this should be a part of the professional teacher's repertoire. A helpful approach is set out by Watkins and Thacker in their 1993 book, *Tutoring*, and the section below is based on this.

What should I do if a degree of conflict is involved?

Conflict needs to be addressed rather than denied or swept under the carpet. Useful steps in outline are:

1. Deal with the feelings first. Parents may be very stirred up and it is helpful to give them room to speak.
2. Use the skills of active listening; reflect back what you hear to signal to the parents that you are trying to understand their viewpoint.
3. Then briefly state your own point of view remembering to separate the person from the issue and avoid general judgmental statements; instead, describe in as accurate and factual way as

possible what concerns you and the effects on yourself and/or other people.

4 Try to arrive at a statement of the problem that incorporates both points of view. The problem can then become a joint problem that you can unite in trying to solve rather than remaining as two separate viewpoints with which you cudgel each other.

This is not easy to do, especially when feelings are high and the steps may take more than one meeting. However, if a sense of trust has been built up between parents and the school in calmer moments and the ethos of the school is one of partnership with parents, it should be possible.

Above all, if you can both signal and recognise that you have the best interests of the student at heart, then these principles should allow you to come to a common formulation of the problem.

It may help to remember that contrasts of viewpoint can be helpful to creativity and that resolving conflicts is tough work.

Finally, this conflict-resolution approach can bring issues out into the open and formulate them as a joint problem where you are both aiming for a win–win solution. This shared problem can now be tackled in the three-step model which we have already discussed (Watkins and Thacker, 1993, p. 187).

Children with a statement of Special Educational Need

For children who have a statement of Special Educational Need, the law requires that an Individual Education Plan (IEP) is drawn up. When drawing up an IEP for a child the classteacher, parents and, where appropriate, the child, should all be involved. At times the adults may need time to discuss things before a child becomes involved. However, the child should have the opportunity, directly or through someone else, to put forward his or her ideas about what works well, whether previous targets have been met, what seems to help and what he or she would like to focus on next. If the child is not at the meeting itself, then an adult should report back to him or her about what was said. This involvement encourages everyone to have an interest in things succeeding.

Sometimes a school-based target is successfully achieved and then parents voice concerns that a similar thing should happen at home.

This enables the school to support the home and allows for the school success to be built on and for consistency to be fostered between home and school. It is important that this is driven by the parents and not by the teachers feeling that 'the home needs to be sorted out'.

Contracts and contacts between home and school

Recent government initiatives such as home–school contracts move towards parents having increased responsibility for their children. However, parents who have difficult children frequently feel deskilled, judged unfavourably and therefore unable to do something about their child's behaviour. Therefore a document highlighting that it is their responsibility and somehow their fault if things go wrong at school may be less than helpful when enshrined in an official home–school contract. That is not to say that parents do not influence and cannot help their children but that the responsibility is a collective one involving school, parents, child and possibly other agencies. We all have a part to play.

At times some people will feel unable to offer anything. It is not uncommon for a parent to feel extremely threatened by coming into school no matter what the school is aiming to do. Just as with the child it is important to remember there will be a reason for the parent's behaviour. This may relate to factors such as the parents' own experiences of school. The importance of building relationships with parents is therefore important. This needs to be done at an early stage and can begin with sending home positive statements about what the child is achieving.

Sometimes, where direct positive communication is difficult, positive statements can be spread via other parents. An example could be that a teacher might say, 'I was really pleased by the way that Peter and Lee worked on their project' to Lee's parents, and they might pass the good news across to Peter's parents outside the school. With this approach the parent, just like some children, may be more willing to hear about success from their peers. The positive effect of a classteacher phoning a parent to share how well his/her son/daughter had done may enable the parent to come into school later in the year in a more relaxed manner. This positive start can then be built upon so that, near the end of the year, if things become difficult for the child in school, the parent will feel that the school is balanced and fair. For some parents home visits can be a helpful way of engaging on safe territory. For others it may be threatening as they may have had previous experiences of professionals working in their home that left them feeling disempowered. It is important that schools do not wait for things to get so difficult that communication becomes impossible.

Joint meetings with child and parents

The use of meetings with parents and child together can be very informative and productive for all concerned. Asking questions of the child which are open-ended, allowing them to share positive statements and set goals in a public arena can trigger change. The teacher may ask: 'What are you pleased with?', 'What have you managed well?', 'When do things go well for you?'. The teacher may then reflect back or search for more depth or clarity – 'Tell me about that?', 'What's that like?', 'You like maths then?'. At times it may be tempting for any of the people involved – child or adult – to want to talk about an event which the child has not managed. There may be a place for this ownership of behaviour to take place but the value of staying positive and letting this be heard and felt by all allows bridges to be built and positive vocabulary to be learned. This can be a strategy to use regularly in meetings with parents or written communication to highlight progress. Using a positive-statements diary to let a parent know, for example, that 'when it was time to pack away, even though he had not finished, he put his work away for next time staying very calm'. Similar statements by parents, in the diary, may illuminate and add depth to the relationship between teacher and child.

What do we do when relations break down?

Understandably, there are times when things break down and it becomes difficult for school and home to communicate appropriately, let alone work together. At such points, or ideally earlier, outside agencies such as educational psychologists can be helpful. As an outsider the psychologist can act as an intermediary between home and school allowing a plan to be worked out for the benefit of the child. In this temporary system the psychologist can enable different ways of perceiving and working to be explored in one class while maintaining good relationships with the rest of the school. This often makes it possible for progress to be made even though other members of staff may have an investment in continuing to see this child as troublesome. For instance, if a teacher has had trouble with a child the previous year, it may be quite wounding to professional pride to see the child improve in another teacher's class. For a further discussion of this complex area the reader should refer to the work of Andy Miller (1996).

Home–school contacts involve children and are not merely the domain of adults. Schools and homes working together can support children to manage differently, even in very challenging situations. Schools need to look at how parents and school staff can together support their children. Teachers need to ensure that they do not blame parents but recognise that parental behaviour is usually motivated by a genuine concern for their children, however misguided this may seem from the perspective of a teacher.

We believe there is not one simple approach to working with parents. We have outlined some ideas that are helpful generally and also strategies for when things are challenging. Schools need to focus largely on what they have control over, which is the school setting. The next chapter looks at the manner in which these systems and approaches need fine-tuning to fit individuals.

Chapter 6

Fine-tuning to support an individual's needs

The previous chapters have highlighted an approach that will enable teachers to work very effectively with most children. We have looked at the teacher who:

- understands the ways in which children with EBD have been thought about and educated over the last several decades (chapter 1);
- is thoughtful of their own attitudes and emotions and who tries to stay positive whilst sticking with difficult situations (chapter 2);
- has a classroom that is well managed and has children working effectively together in groups (chapter 3);
- is in a school which is supportive, imaginative and flexible (chapter 4);
- works in a context where there is a thoughtful home–school interface (chapter 5).

Such a teacher may well find that children who have previously been categorised as EBD elsewhere no longer need to be compartmentalised or isolated by this label. This chapter is about how a teacher can build upon these secure foundations over time to fine-tune his or her approach to an individual child. Fine-tuning learning to meet an individual's needs is not unusual and should also be done for a child with EBD. In the same way, we believe that learning about personal and social issues should also be fine-tuned to meet the needs of any individual. This chapter looks at what fine-tuning may entail and highlights the major processes that are likely to be involved:

- building a relationship;
- monitoring and owning behaviour;
- setting targets;
- 'sticking with it';
- learning from mistakes;
- refocusing targets and increasing expectations in line with others in the group;
- moving away from fine-tuning when appropriate, back towards working with the whole group in general terms so that the child can 'lose their label'.

What is fine-tuning and why is it important?

Let us look at a concrete example to illustrate the process. For example, a child is hurting people at break-times and the teacher decides that action is necessary. The child may be illuminating the system's shortfalls such as lack of clear expectations, poor opportunities for play or lack of skills/knowledge of games, and appropriate action may need to be taken on any or all these fronts. In addition to more general action which might involve making better provision for play, fine-tuning for the child might involve the teacher sitting down with the individual before break-time asking what game to play, whom to play it with and how to ask for help if the child encounters a difficulty. A similar conversation might be held with the child and a small number of friends. In another case it may be appropriate for a learning support assistant to help engineer a play situation. In this way, the child can give us an opportunity for fine-tuning the systems we operate within and allow us to improve the situation for all children in the class/school.

For situations which do not require immediate action, we should allow children time to blend into their class and experience the emotions which they naturally feel when a group is forming. We have already seen in chapter 3 how groups and individuals in them go through a variety of stages including 'storming' as part of an expected part of classroom life.

Adults and children tend to be more sympathetic when the child concerned has difficulties occurring from more visible disabilitites, such as Down's syndrome or being in a wheelchair, but when the child has the label EBD there may be fear of the label, making such work with the class group particularly important for children with EBD. A whole-class approach using group work can help the class to realise why a child needs support and may also show the class that an individual child may need different expectations. We saw an example of this in a case study which we looked at in chapter 3. There (pp. 70–74) Elly describes a group work session which provided an opportunity for the rest of the class to explore how they felt about a new entrant, Miles, since 'he was meeting more and more situations that challenged his autistic tendencies and children and adults were getting physically hurt by him'. She set up a group work session when Miles was out of the room and together they shared their responses to the prompt 'Is there anything you noticed that you didn't like or understand?'. As Elly reports:

> the floodgates opened and a picture of huge complexity emerged. There were jealousies, there were fears, and there were genuine triumphs and celebrations. As we shared in the circle there were connections drawn between some of Miles's behaviour and the tantrums that younger brothers and sisters had.

This 'reframing' by Elly was followed by

> . . . a round of our own worst toddler anecdotes. Somehow bringing his behaviour in line with our own put a more human face on things. Each of us was still capable of 'throwing a wobbly'. It was just we hardly ever did it, whereas Miles did it all the time.

This reframing helped the children to see Miles's behaviour as amusing rather than frightening and Elly reports that she

> was surprised to hear all the positive suggestions about how to manage alongside an irritable toddler. The session finished with the prompt, 'Now that I've talked, I feel . . .' and 'I'm going to try *x* when *y* happens'.

This is not an easy option for the class members or the teacher as it is likely to require different ways of working. But it can lead to insights about what helps and can help the class to understand why one child may need this sort of help at first while most other children can access school experiences with minimal support.

Elastic boundaries

The teacher has to find the balance between individual and class needs. A fine-tuning approach is not about isolating an individual child but about using elastic boundaries and expectations that will allow the child the opportunity to be outside the expectations for the others in the class group for the moment, but will nevertheless draw the child back towards the group. There may be very particular reasons why a child might need such allowances. A child, for example, who is scared by large groups may find assemblies too much, or one who has been through a traumatic fire may be greatly affected by a fire practice.

Far less dramatic but equally important is the child who is not developmentally ready to work within the rest of the class's expectations, although the child is certainly a part of the class. Many aspects of school are age-related, e.g. the age of starting school, but teachers know that some children may have missed out on crucial experiences and thus be lagging behind their age-peers in certain aspects of their development. For example some new entrants may have been regularly read to and as a consequence have developed a wide vocabulary and a pleasure in books. In the same class there may be others who, not having had this experience, may not have gained such a wide vocabulary or see books in such a positive light.

These differences can feel greater as the child gets older. For example, it is not uncommon for teachers to work with children who have been categorised as gifted in their school attainments but who have little social awareness of their peers. The child may be able to get by within the primary school but is he or she prepared for the secondary school with its very different, multi-teacher approach? Such tensions are not easily resolved but they need to be addressed to find the best fit available for the child at any particular time.

The elasticity of boundaries may need to happen for short or for long periods of time, according to need. It is not suggested that the child will never manage with the ordinary demands of the class, but that this could be a problem some time in the future. Sometimes we hear it said that the child knows the expectations and it is now his or her responsibility to blend in. We view this as often unrealistic and unfair, although this is not to excuse the behaviour or say that the child will never be able to change. Children may need help and support to see the purpose of such expectations and to learn how to manage differently.

Building a relationship

The basic requirement for any work with children with EBD is to build a relationship with that child. Challenging children tend to find it harder to relate easily to their teacher and/or their peer group. As relationships develop, children can access the opportunities for learning more readily. When a child is working with an adult with whom they feel safe, much more is possible. The following short extract from Dave's case study of his work with Darren highlights the difference that such an adult can make.

> An interesting example of the way Darren presented himself occurred at the end of Year 5 (aged nine) when an educational psychologist came in to do some assessments relating to his cognitive abilities as the need for looking at future schooling was arising. To my surprise, whilst I knew his levels of attainment were not good, I believed he had something about him that was bright and quick-thinking. The tests, however, showed him to be within the moderate-learning-difficulties band. This also surprised the people at the children's home where he lived. At the beginning of the next academic year Darren was retested with a different educational psychologist. I asked if I could sit in on the assessment as I thought it might affect the way he worked. This time he came out as average on the test and I still felt Darren was playing games once he got bored.

The skilled teacher tries to build positive relationships with all children. For some children this may take more effort or time. All teachers will recognise children they 'click' with and others whom they never really get to know as well. Finding a child's interest can be helpful and a common or shared interest can build a bridge. The importance of greeting children in the mornings and saying goodbye at the end of the day can also help in this area. Touch, linked to praise, can be a helpful way of improving behaviour through reassuring someone that they are OK and you are supportive of them (Wheldall *et al.*, 1986). The use of touch may not feel comfortable for all teachers or children. There are risks associated with touching children at all because of public concern over child abuse but we would argue for the importance of appropriate touch in the process of working with children.

Some children may 'act out' in order to see if you are a safe adult. Will you just shout at them? Jessie Taft comments: 'The child with emotional and behavioural difficulties . . . want[s] someone wise enough not to be fooled and strong enough not to retaliate' (paraphrase of Jessie Taft cited in Moustakas, 1959). Once children know you are not scared away by such behaviour they will feel safer and can change more readily. Such children need the teacher, as an important adult, to keep valuing them and what they do. The teacher also needs to hold boundaries so that the child can feel safe and know what to expect. By an adult building a bridge towards the child, the child can begin to get a sense of someone else's world through a person he or she trusts. The relationship is vital and all else follows on from this. If the child has such a relationship to build from, even when things go wrong or are difficult between adult and child, the intention behind the relationship will be seen. The child, seeing the adult's poor choice of intervention, is more likely to recognise that the adult was trying, albeit unsuccessfully, to get it right for her or him.

The importance of all relationships, and not just adult–child relationships, underpins much of our approach as highlighted in chapter 3. Group work helps children to link with their peers and for the child with a label to be seen more positively. It also allows all the children to get to know the teacher as a person and not just in his or her role of teacher. The fact that the teacher has interests and worries and celebrations is important in the relationship-building process which is a two-way process and not just about the teacher getting to know the child.

Monitoring and ownership

As the relationship between a teacher and a child develops it becomes more possible for change to occur. As a precursor to a change in behaviour, the teacher might expect a stage where the positive aspects of a situation and sometimes the difficulties can be recognised, monitored and subsequently named. The naming alone can change things. This process is as true for the teacher as for the child. It is important for children to build an awareness of how their environment is influencing them and what it is that they do that is having an effect on others around them. Some children are able to list their negative behaviours but are not able to highlight the things that they can do well. The latter skill is particularly important if we are to build solutions rather than to be drawn into problems.

Monitoring by the teacher

Monitoring by the teacher gives an opportunity to fine-tune the learning environment for both the class and the individuals within it. The peer group are as much a part of the context as the individual in terms of seeking to improve the situation. The teacher, when looking to support an individual, needs to examine the effects of the child's environment.

- How are children affected by the peer group?
- By the design of the classroom?
- By whom they work with?
- Are particular times of the day difficult?

By carefully monitoring and observing the child in context it may be possible to see ways of adapting the environment to help support individuals within the school. Supporting individuals, perhaps through improved differentiation or more (or less) accessible resources, may actually benefit a number of children. These benefits can be direct where the change initiated for one individual also helps another. It may also help less directly where, by a child managing more easily, the whole group can function in a different kind of way. Systemic thinking allows us to look at a range of options to support, from a traditional viewpoint, one member of a group. If we remember that the child's behaviour may be highlighting things that others may be feeling, then these children can be seen as a great opportunity. They aid us in improving things for other children. What may appear a piece of fine-tuning for one child may actually be a lot less individualistic than we think.

Since behaviour is influenced by the context, a number of environmental factors (from classroom management to a whole-school reward scheme, to peer relationships) can be used to support the situation. However, it is sometimes tempting, after gaining insight from observations, to try to change everything at once. It is wiser to change things gradually so that the effect of each change can be observed and changes sustained. The importance of the luxury of watching your own class should not be underestimated. Being released by another colleague to do this could be a helpful way of schools being able to take ownership of difficult situations rather than referring to the expert straight away. The above does carry some resourcing implications but it may be money very well spent.

Monitoring in groups

Monitoring can be done in class or small groups. The whole group method of monitoring provides a way of each member of the group giving feedback to the others. Work that relates to specific incidents, such as bullying, can be explored in general terms through group work and drama. A round of 'how you feel when someone spoils a game at playtime' gives all children the chance to voice their feelings and for them to understand the impact of some behaviours without it becoming a personal attack on one person. Similarly, through the use of role play or soliloquy to an imaginary bully feelings, ideas and strategies can be explored. The use of group work to reflect on a range of issues is helpful for children to gain awareness of themselves and other children within their class.

Involving the peer group through regular reflection in group work allows both teacher and pupil to think through, in a safe and structured manner, when things went well, when they didn't, what they would like to happen and strategies for achieving this. As trust builds up in groups then children can help one another by offering feedback. This does not have to relate to times when things went wrong, but could focus on when it was good to work with a partner or ways in which someone helped in the classroom.

Self-monitoring

Monitoring of behaviour should not be solely the realm of adults or the peer group. A child should be encouraged to monitor his/her own behaviour to help build an awareness of it. While it may be easier to highlight how awful he/she has been, it is important to keep looking for the positives. Teachers should encourage children to think about what things went well and what helped them to turn out that way. Monitoring may be general or focused upon a particular behaviour. In the latter it is important to monitor something positive such as putting a hand up for attention rather than calling out. For general self-monitoring a rating system of how a child has done may be useful. Perhaps having colours or symbols for the child to highlight what he/she think is good, OK, and not OK could be used in a lesson? The teacher can discuss the children's record with them and highlight what they themselves thought they did to get good result. By discussing when things went well a child is given a positive language for discussing his/her achievements, playing down the child's negative self-image. Such an approach will not work for every child and much of its success will depend upon the child's ability to feel that this is part of a scheme to help rather than to persecute him or her.

What if the child needs the attention?

The use of monitoring for behaviours such as calling out during lessons may be complicated if the underlying reason behind the behaviour is a need for attention. It is worth remembering some attention, even if it is negative, is better than none at all for a number of children. For such children there is no motivation for them to change their behaviour if the teacher already constantly engages with them through telling them off or talking things through. In this situation the child should be encouraged only to monitor when things went well and the teacher should not enter into discussions about what things went wrong (no matter how tempting!).

What if the behaviour is dangerous?

In the case of behaviours, such as violence, that the teacher cannot choose to ignore because of the safety of other children, an attempt should be made to resolve the situation and finish with what the child could do next time to prevent such a situation happening again. This process may not be achieved in one go but only over a period of time. It is also important for the teacher, even in situations where the child's behaviour cannot be ignored, to consider, 'Am I being drawn into the problem rather than building the solution?'

Interviewing children

In all this work, it is helpful if the teacher does not judge what she or he hears but just listens carefully to the child. The way we question children is important and 'What?' and 'How?' questions are more likely to get answers than 'Why?'. Asking a child 'What happened?'

is easier to answer than 'Why did you do that?'; and if the child is unable to say we may need to listen to other children's accounts of what happened. It is important that everyone has the chance to tell their story. A framework provided by the teacher such as 'What happened?', 'What would you have liked to have happened?', 'What can be done to resolve the situation?' may help. This is helpful in giving a picture and may allow the child to build an awareness of the impact of his/her behaviour. This awareness may be helped where 'I' statements are used in order to separate the person from the behaviour. An example would be if, following a playground argument, one child heard another child say, 'I got worried when you shouted at me because I thought you might hurt me'. Our experience is that hearing other people's vulnerabilities, whether child or adult, does not result in these admissions being used against that person later. These statements may help the child to make important connections.

When 'ownership' is difficult

Some children may feel unable to 'objectively' own their behaviour. They may have insufficient relationship with the teacher, be fearful of consequences or be adjusting their picture of the world extremely quickly to protect their self-concept. For others there may be difficulties in processing experience. However, this stage of building awareness is important and, as significant relationships develop, it seems possible for all to acknowledge that they have a part to play and can all work together.

However, ownership may be complicated by a lack of knowledge of how to change. The child needs to learn that actions have consequences but that, by facing these consequences with adult or peer facilitation and questioning, solutions and ways of resolving things can be found. Some children may find this difficult at first and have no ideas, so the teacher may need to offer some suggestions or ask other children what they think could be done to resolve things. This lack of ideas may not be obtuseness, as some teachers see it, or even fear of what may happen but quite simply a lack of knowledge resulting from not meeting such a process previously and therefore having no bank of ideas to work from. As children build up their resource-bank of solutions they may suggest saying sorry or doing something for someone. This process is not static. At first saying sorry may involve a huge leap forward for a child.

Later this may not be enough and the child will need to do more to 'put things right'. We have all experienced a person saying sorry and felt that this was an amazing step forward, just as we have all experienced the opposite, when 'sorry' means nothing at all. By the adult not blaming the child, encouraging him/her to find solutions and offering possibilities when the child gets stuck, then solutions can be discovered.

Target-setting

Target-setting may be a general approach that is used with children as outlined in chapter 3. This could involve children setting themselves targets for the next half term concerning school generally or be focused on a particular aspect of schooling such as literacy or break-times. Targets could be for individuals or for the whole class. There is not one right way but each will certainly carry different benefits and difficulties for members of the class.

The whole class can sometimes benefit when situations are set up to fine-tune a target for an individual child. For instance, the child who finds it impossible to take turns listening to others in a group can take ownership for himself during a whole-class focus on the question, 'What can each of us do to improve the quality of whole class discussions?'. This group reflection can avoid a personal focus on the child. Another non-threatening way to fine-tune target-setting for individuals can be by the use of class partners giving each other feedback. Prompts like 'I am pleased with my work on *x* but I would like to get better at *y*' and 'How do you think I could do this?' may be useful. Teacher and child become partners in this way, sounding out ideas and strategies together, with the child taking as much responsibility as he/ she is ready for.

The child who is encouraged to work towards resolving difficulties and setting targets can join together with parents and teacher to take an active part in drawing up an IEP. IEPs should not have too many targets, no more than three, and, as already discussed, these should be broken down so that everyone is clear about what they are trying to do and how this can be achieved. Just because the IEP is, as its name suggests, individual does not take away the systemic context, that is, part of a plan which may involve work individually, in groups, in class or not even involve the child at all. An example of this last point might involve MTAs setting up play situations at lunchtimes to support all children or the teacher using group work to look at how it feels when you are left out. We are trying through the IEP to meet a child's needs and this can be done in a range of different ways.

Later in this chapter the case study of Elly and Miles examines such a situation in detail. Through the teacher listening without judgement and with thoughtful questioning, the child can be helped to reflect and think ahead. Teachers can support a child's learning without telling him or her the answers. Indeed, for some children, by the teacher saying what they think should happen, the strategy is automatically set for failure. At times the teacher may wish to push the child in one particular direction because of the difficulties that she or he has. The child may already be aware of the difficulties the teacher is noticing, and will suggest this as an area that she/he could produce as a target, especially if a joint problem-solving approach is being used (see, for example, Thacker, 1983).

If the child doesn't suggest this, then having one teacher-driven target and one child-driven target may be a useful compromise. Target-setting is not necessarily about reaching a level of 'just managing' in class. With a teacher providing guidance, resources and opportunities the child can set him- or herself high targets and pass milestones which others might have thought too ambitious for him or her. Being seen in a positive light can release a child from previous constraints and awaken the view that 'anything is possible'. The child who is invited to set his/her own best-wish target may choose a seemingly unreachable aim. The skill of the adult comes in breaking down the target into manageable and observable chunks and planning strategies to enable the child's motivation and energy to succeed. It is easier to 'learn a different times table each week' than to 'improve my maths' or even the more focused version of 'improve my tables'. It is common for children to say 'I will improve my behaviour' or 'I'll never do that again'. Such statements reinforce failure as it is unrealistic for the child to change everything at once. Once the child has been guided through this process of choosing a target, breaking it up into bite-sized pieces and deciding what the success criteria will be, it may be possible to repeat the process with less support. Through practice children can learn this process for themselves. As Lodge and Watkins (1999) point out, such children are being encouraged to learn about learning. They also highlight potential difficulties with target-setting that should be borne in mind where we become too focused upon 'outcomes' and 'measures'. These difficulties may include a narrowed curriculum, focusing on some children and not others, seeking to include some and exclude others and the increase of blame if targets do not get met. However, by enabling the child to create a vision whereby things can be different, then change is more likely to occur and be recognised when it does. Creative visualisation can be a powerful tool for achieving this with whole classes of children (see e.g. Hall *et al.*, 1990).

Teachers can help children think through where potential difficulties could arise and what can be done if they are encountered. The use of peer support could be helpful where a child is finding it difficult to manage and the rest of the class can try and encourage the child to manage/meet his or her targets. By the targets being positive, as outlined above, then it is possible for teacher and peer group to congratulate individuals when they are doing well. If the target is negative, such as 'I won't swear', then the focus becomes swearing rather than speaking politely. Naturally we tend to notice only when things go wrong and so reinforce the problem. We are then quite likely to be building up the swearing rather than decreasing it.

Working with other adults

When situations become difficult it is often necessary for the teacher to work with other people. Fine-tuning your everyday processes may be necessary when working with some parents. This may simply involve the flexibility of meeting late after school to allow for a parent's work commitments, or could go further and involve a teacher regularly ringing a parent to inform them of their child's progress. However, as suggested in the previous chapter, it is important for schools to work with parents at an early stage, ideally when things are going well, and not wait for things to break down. Parents should be involved in the designing of IEPs alongside the classteacher, and where appropriate (age, confidence and group size) the child and possibly the SENCo. If the classteacher has the responsibility for writing the IEP it becomes possible for the SENCo, doing what their title implies, to coordinate rather than doing everything for everyone else. Such an approach allows teachers, parents and, as we shall see, children, to be involved in such work. Such a process allows everyone to share in success when things go well and support one another if mistakes are made. When teachers get stuck it is important that they are willing to go for support. However, they should not be too quick off the blocks otherwise they avoid learning themselves. The best interventions by educational psychologists support teachers by helping them find their own answers rather than the quick fix of 'do this and monitor for half a term'. Educational psychologists and advisory staff have a wealth of knowledge and experience to share, and they can create a temporary system with a classteacher where different ideas can be tried out safely for a period of time. This approach is explored further in Miller (1996).

No matter how many different adults are involved it is important that the child remains involved and central to the process. Support should, wherever possible, involve the child and not be something that is done to him/her. Whether this is monitoring, target-setting or meeting with parents to prepare an IEP, the child should be involved at every step. Where it would not be productive for a child, for example, to sit in on a meeting with the teacher and parent(s), collating a child's ideas beforehand would be helpful. Similarly at the end a potted version of the meeting can be given to the child. We need to work towards the child being able to manage in such meetings for him- or herself. In all cases, we involve the child as fully as he or she is able.

Sticking with it

It is important, as teachers, that we try ideas out, adapt things if they go wrong and not be too rigid to try a different tack. We must also be resilient as change may take time. The teacher who says 'I've already done that' may not have done it in the same way as yourself. A simple adaptation or different relationship can make all the difference. We all change and sometimes coming back to the same strategy that earlier had been unproductive may work well second time around. The teacher's willingness to stay positive with the child and the situation and stick with this is very important.

Quite often we are amazed how, just at the point when things seem at their lowest ebb and everyone feels like giving up, the greatest opportunities for change and learning can occur. The tenacity of the teacher to stick around until these changes occur is an ability that few outside teaching may fully recognise or appreciate.

The importance of teacher attributes such as flexibility, being reflective, having empathy for the child and good communication skills become as important as the actual strategy itself. The teacher who has not worked at these is more likely to give up when things get difficult. The teacher who can work at these, and avoid blaming, is likely to separate the individual's behaviour from the individual, thus avoiding things becoming personal. This allows the teacher to sustain their efforts.

The more teachers engage with the processes outlined in this book, the more likely they are to recognise some of the markers we have described. It is not about set answers and so knowing what to do next but about recognising the truth of things such as 'I felt like this last time, not knowing what to do, but I came out the other side'. Through reflection on our processes we are more likely to feel safe with the challenges that face us and enable ourselves to stick with the difficulties or see things differently. Such an approach leads to a teacher realising that it is fine not to know the answer or to have chosen the wrong strategy. This is merely part of making the context better.

As things become tough the ability to stay calm and not take an authoritarian role is challenging. The ability to be able to deliver the strategy in a positive and calm manner is vital if we are not to reinforce previously learned patterns of behaviour. Often when children do not get the expected response from an adult they increase the intensity of their behaviour. The child who is ignored when he or she calls out and then sees the teacher praise other children for putting their hand up may react by calling out louder. The teacher then has to choose to stick with this strategy and ride the storm or to change tack or adapt what they are doing. There is no set answer for every occasion. The teacher may find that he or she can no longer choose to ignore the behaviour of a child. At such times it is important that we recognise our own emotions. Some children will push and push until they get their needs met, often with a strong teacher reaction. If the situation arises where things need to be stated then it is important for the statement to be delivered calmly, so that the child hears the message rather than seeing the teacher's irritation. By staying calm the teacher may already be challenging what the child has previously learnt about the way adults react. The child is also, if they see the adult as an advocate, likely to hear the realness of a statement such as 'I'm finding it really difficult when you call out because I feel nobody else can hear me'. For much of this book we have highlighted how helpful it is to stay positive but it is also true that much learning can come from seeing negative experiences in a different way. Unfortunately what too often happens is that the focus tends to become completely negative and so the impact of possible learning from these statements is lost. By being predominantly positive a 'real' statement about something you are finding difficult is likely to carry impact.

Making mistakes

It can actually be productive to get things wrong and learning from these mistakes can help us to get it better in the future. It would be surprising if, with something as complex as teaching, we never made mistakes. The teacher who tries to cover his tracks in such situations not only blocks his own learning but models for children that getting it wrong is not helpful. Teachers need to consider how much they need to control and what is their reason for controlling. By letting things happen and letting mistakes get worked through, teachers can enable children to learn a great deal about operating in a group. This is not an easy decision for teachers, who are accountable, to make for their classrooms. We feel that at times teachers actually stop this learning from happening by their interventions. This may result in things temporarily being OK, but it does not really sort out the underlying issues. Children are sometimes stopped from working and learning by teacher input that may be inappropriate or too frequent. When children are 'in flow' then part of a teacher's skill is to let that continue rather than damming the process.

Refocusing and increasing expectations

Part of the monitoring and target-setting cycle that we are proposing is the ability to review how things have gone so that we can celebrate the efforts made and so that targets can be adapted, refocused or newly invented. As with other parts of the cycle, it is important for all, including the child, to be involved.

Once a child has made progress it is tempting to sit back and heave a sigh of relief that he or she no longer calls out or hits people, etc. However, it is important for the elasticity of the boundaries to operate and pull the child back towards the expectations that the teacher holds of others. By such refocusing, further fine-tuning may be necessary to support the child in blending in with the class. Eventually a stage is reached when we can consider the child to be within the normal range of the class. Here such conscious fine-tuning can stop in order to allow the child to 'lose' his/her label.

'Losing the label' can sometimes take time and involve group support so that everyone is aware that such individual support and flexibility is no longer a necessity. Reflecting back how it used to be can help a child to realise the success he or she has made. A round with a class of something that Wayne has improved on, can help Wayne realise that he can now play a different role in class. This need not only be done for Wayne but could be part of a weekly cycle of celebrations about class members.

For some children there is no tidy ending and so the stages of sticking with it and refocusing of targets may need to be continued over a long period. Although it may never become easy, we need to remind ourselves of what progress is being made.

Case studies

We finish with a number of case studies which illustrate aspects of fine-tuning. The courses of action, quite obviously, vary from individual to individual. As such the ideas expressed in these cases are not about how useful a particular strategy is but about the flexibility, thought and aim to find the best fit that underpins our work with a child.

Fine-tuning Elly and Miles

There were several 'taken for granted' attitudes in place when the head welcomed eight-year-old Miles midway through the school year, but there was no specific staff knowledge about any of his disabilities. He was partially sighted, hemiplegic and with autistic tendencies. This work would be new territory for all of us but the head had listened to his story and declared he would be 'a gift to the school'. This was a great act of faith since he had not even met the boy but was based on the sort of risk-taking on which many of us thrived.

Oddly, I knew more about his mother and her reputation on the inter-schools grapevine than I did about Miles. She had a name for fighting for her son's rights and was quietly yet inexorably determined when she met an obstacle or an injustice. On the other hand, she was no novice and had worked miracles for Miles since his adoption as a baby, and I felt she would be the best resource that I could have in getting to know him. At the start I made a conscious effort to build up trust and acceptance between us. She was not easy to get to know and was always fairly private, but I had the impression of a person who was willing to give us a chance. Dave as SENCo called a meeting for us all to talk about how Miles was settling in, but it looked as if it would be impossible for the father to be there because of working away from home. An after-school meeting was also difficult because Miles was not used to baby-sitters or going to other children's houses and his routines were very important. It seemed natural for Dave and I to offer to visit the home after Miles had gone to bed. This really took them by surprise but I think it went a long way towards establishing a good relationship between the four of us. I believe that Miles's mother and father felt valued because we arranged the meeting on their terms and that we listened to their story so far and asked for their advice on relating to Miles.

A second meeting, similar time and place, took them further by surprise when Dave produced an IEP form and asked them for their thoughts and aspirations. It felt as if we were collaborating on equal terms and each of us fed back our observations of Miles and gave our immediate plans for him in school.

Dave was SENCo but also a good colleague for me to talk through strategies with and also celebrate successes. Although our experiences and backgrounds were very different, we shared a common belief in children and their parents.

Miles's parents expressed surprise that they could take such an active part in setting his IEP. In other schools they had been involved in IEP interviews where they had had the chosen (by staff) targets carefully explained to them. They felt that our procedure was significantly different for them.

Some months passed and Miles was becoming more aware of himself and of his place in the group. It felt time to involve him more fully in target-setting for his IEP and we decided to meet after school – just Miles, his mother and myself. In reviewing his previous IEP there were positives to feed back and as his mother and I reported our pleasure in his achievements he met our comments with his own delightful brand of flustered modesty. It had taken time and effort to help him listen to and receive even positive feedback. He seemed to need copious amounts of detail in order to understand, and his constant but genuine questioning helped me to give a much clearer explanation of his progress in which I actually named the skills he had mastered. Instead of saying 'I'm pleased how you've learned to come in to the classroom without disturbing others', I had to give a much fuller account. Being partially sighted, he never stood at the doorway and cast a glance around the room to find out what was going on among each group of children (something we do automatically with good sight). A day course run by the advisory service had highlighted this for me and I had thought hard about how to alter Miles's anti-social habit of blasting noisily into a room and aggressively shoving children aside, demanding to know what they were doing. I had broken this down into stages and was able to explain to him: 'I'm pleased that you have learned to stop and listen at the doorway, to walk to your place, to say "Excuse me, would you mind explaining what you are busy doing?" to anyone you notice and to stand and listen to what they tell you. I'm pleased that you realise that they are concentrating and that you need to do this quietly and carefully. I'm also pleased that, almost always, you then find your work and start doing it with your classroom assistant.' This detail also served to put his mother in the picture and it showed us all that we had gone through a process in reaching the target. When it was time for Miles to review what he felt he had achieved, he said it was his drawing. Now he was already an excellent pen-and-ink artist but I felt equally able to question him for more details: 'How have you improved?', 'What can you do now that you couldn't do before?', 'What helped you?'. In a mirror image of my own explanation he told me the skills he had acquired and the way these had built up for him. After the review each of us put forward a target idea. Of course Miles stuck to familiar territory. He was not yet a risk-taker and knew how to look after his own interests! I could have put forward so many ideas – behavioural and academic – but this needed to be one step at a time and Miles needed to be respected. It took a succession of short-term targets, mainly on his own terms, before he trusted the process and I felt I could ease him towards bigger challenges. He was very creative in suggesting criteria for success and in ways of monitoring progress and was very fair indeed with rewards and sanctions. I had to be flexible and innovative in order to maintain his interest and motivation, but I think that the whole machinery of change always went relentlessly forward. If a target was not achieved we still talked about it supportively and tried to see whether it was clear enough or whether there was enough support. Could it be returned to at a different date? Could we think of a more helpful route? For Miles with his gift for language and his autistic tendencies there had to be clear information and an open and generous dialogue. His parents gave us good advice when they told us early on that he would always win an argument, and confronting him was not the way forward.

It was important not to be frightened of Miles when he flew into a rage and hit and hurled anything within reach. He was panicked and frustrated by many things and I learned quickly not always to identify what had triggered off his anger or even to respond to it but to be brave enough to reflect back that I knew he must be feeling very cross. Of course, some of the time he could not be allowed to hurt other children and adults but it worked both ways and he was often teased or goaded into actions at break-times by others. I was determined to be fair but elastic, and little by little we acted out the way to do things using model pirates whilst struggling to face the children he had hurt and finding a way to make things better for them. I think he learned best when he was on the receiving end of such conflict resolution and could hear children checking out if he was OK and trying to convey their apologies for winding him up or pushing him about.

As his mother began to trust that we were still his advocates whatever he did and that our aim was to support him no matter how challenging things were, Miles came step by step to understanding this too. At first in class he seemed oblivious to the fact that other children had feelings and needs, and I thought it would be valuable for him to spend some time each day working with him on this. I introduced a 'Feelings Book' and his classroom assistant explored with him, at a very basic level, 'I feel happy when . . .' and 'I feel sad when . . .', asking Miles to draw pictures and complete sentences. After a while we looked for some intensity of feelings and encouraged him to order them and make observations about facial expressions. In class I was able to mirror what he had worked on when I spoke to him – insisting on eye contact first. 'I feel happy because you have this maths correct: look at my eyes and the muscles in my face, etc.' and 'I feel sad because I just heard you swear at Lyn and I know that has upset her. See my face now . . .'. After a while he got used to this and I could hand over some of the control to him with questions such as: 'What do you notice about my face?', 'How do you think I'm feeling at the moment?' and 'Can you think why?'. Of course he learned about the happy before the sad but he did learn and quite soon took over the 'Feelings Book' for his own purposes. If he came into school in the morning hissing and snapping, unable to communicate with anyone and obviously angry he would quickly take up the suggestion to draw in his book and afterwards go and lie down and talk to himself with his toy soldiers or a reading book. He began to voice powerful feelings of resentment and jealousy in his book. However, I felt this was far more appropriate than in the family or class arena.

Dave, as teacher of the support group as well as SENCo, had been toying with a strategy to help Miles with his extreme temper tantrums at school. When frustrated or frightened Miles would become physically violent, shouting, snarling and hitting out. He often turned his anger on himself and hurled his glasses across the room and bit himself. He seemed frightened by his own anger and strength and exasperated beyond help. Dave decided to cradle him through the next tantrum. He knew how to hold in an enclosing way without hurting Miles and how to use his strength to ride the storm of emotion from him. Miles's mother listened to what we proposed and seemed surprised but not shaken and said that no one had ever tried that before but that we could give it a go. I had a strong sense that she was trusting us now. One day as Miles launched himself into an episode in the nurture group Dave did as he had said and found that, when the rage eventually subsided, Miles was looking up at him and seemed to relax and consider what it felt like to be held. With nothing and no one damaged this time he could get up when he was ready and talk to Dave about something else. (As we saw in the part of the case study of Miles in chapter 4 Elly went on to use the technique in the ordinary class.)

Quite apart from targets in IEPs there were class routines which Miles was coaxed towards managing. He was gifted in reading and writing, although he always played safe in his choice of writing style. At eight years old in Year 3 he was functioning at a good Level 3 in the National Curriculum. Sometimes he wrote himself, sometimes on the keyboard and when tired he would dictate to a scribe. Physically writing was difficult for him with his hemiplegia and nystagmus.

It was part of our class routine to have editing partners and to interview each other using a range of questions to offer ways forward in writing. The questions were a range of affirmations such as 'I like the way you've chosen to use alliteration here', to challenges such as 'As the reader I wanted to know more about what your character looked like. Can you put in some more sentences or adjectives in here to help me?'. Spelling, grammar and verb tenses were also highlighted where possible and then the writer went to work on a second draft. These were higher-order skills for Year 3 and 4 children, but we had begun the year at a quite basic level and were building up skills and successes throughout the year.

Miles hated knowing he had made a spelling mistake and refused point blank to ever look a second time at anything he had written. He often flew into a rage and ripped up a story if anybody made a critical comment. He behaved as though he was very offended and defended himself verbally in the hopes that any marauding critics would be too frightened to return for a second attack.

Mindful of how holding Miles through anger tantrums was enabling him to face the anxiety or fear and eventually address it, I wondered if academic tantrums would be similar. I thought a lot about it and then decided to approach things from a different angle. Could I help him to take my role and become an editor himself? I had no intention of letting him do this with another child because he would be brutally honest and destroy confidence without realising what effect he was having on others. I became his partner and dashed off a really faulty piece of writing and invited him to help me to improve it. At first I pretended that I couldn't possibly change anything. Then I allowed myself to be persuaded. Miles was very brutal indeed but very thorough. He took a rather gloating pleasure in correcting and improving things and I was relieved that I had put myself as a guinea-pig. I fed back to him afterwards my admiration for his skill but did not neglect to tell him how I felt emotionally. He was set a challenge next time to think of a different way to take care of me as well as my mistakes. The next piece of writing I produced was National Curriculum Level 3 and he pushed it back at me with no annotations. It was obviously what he believed was as good as I could get and, when I thought about it, was the sort of writing he was adamantly defending for himself. I had to complain myself that I wasn't happy with my use of adjectives in the description of the setting – how could I paint a more realistic picture? It was the start for him and he began to dig deeper. Over time he built up skills and was more able to articulate different styles of language. His own writing material matured and he could sometimes listen to child-to-child feedback from his classroom assistant and teacher. Towards the end of the next term he produced a stunning piece of descriptive writing inspired by a visit to the beach with his classroom assistant. As he wrote up his second version of it on the computer, he discussed editorial points with his classroom assistant and adjusted what he wanted to say. I assessed the end product at National Curriculum Level 4.

Fine-tuning Elly and Karen

Karen was different in that she suddenly presented with a problem in class, although, if I think about it, there were symptoms there for several days leading up to the change in her behaviour. I'd never thought of her as anything but a bright, bouncy, helpful and sensitive child. She had begun to daydream a bit and was losing interest in her friends and her work and was holding herself on the edge of things and watching me more carefully than usual.

The moment that I noticed that she had disappeared from class my brain began to start making all sorts of connections, but I was still none the wiser. The room was buzzing with a fact-finding session on the Romans revolving around the recent arrival of brand-new glossy library books. Children were busy and excited, working in twos and threes or on their own using indexes and glossaries to make notes for their projects. As I went round in an 'overseeing' role I had half an eye to finding Karen who had not actually left the room. The children were, by this stage of the term, respectful of each other's needs and, although I think they knew I always had time for them as individuals, there was a growing acceptance that if one of them needed me more, they were able to hold back and catch me when there was a space for them. Because of this, when I found Karen in a quiet oasis under a display table curtained by a cloth, I was able to sit with her. I was aware of one or two children approaching during the time I was there, but they reassured themselves that I needed to be there and found alternative solutions to their problems.

'How are you doing? I missed you. Do you need me to help?'

'I want to be dead.'

'Do you?'

'Yes, I should be dead.'

She sat, curled up as tight as she could get under the cloth.

'But you're not dead. You're here in class with me and your friends.'

'Nobody likes me. I want to be dead.'

Well, what do you do? She was certainly not playing a game. She could not be cheered up. She was clearly quite disturbed.

My first instinct was to suggest I talk to her mother and tell her how she was feeling at school. She accepted this readily and said that she wanted her mum to know but that I had to tell her.

This was the start of eighteen months' hard work for her mother, the social worker and the clinical psychologist as well as for me and the class.

School was probably the only safe place for this child to start making her needs known and, although she shared me with thirty-three other children, I was a trusted adult who had not been directly affected by her trauma in the summer holidays. I spent six and a half hours, five days a week with her and she wanted to involve me. I recognised my role here and quickly connected the family to the appropriate professionals. Although not dealing directly with the subject of the trauma the behaviours which resulted from it were in class with me daily and were there for me to experience as a teacher.

Karen and her family had been pulled out of the wreckage of an horrendous car crash and she had been the only one to be relatively unscathed. Her mother was now safely alive, another passenger was making a partial recovery, and two other children were having nightmares but gradually getting over it. Karen had kept them all going. Everyone had praised her for being brave, grown up, motherly and cheerful. They thought she had survived the ordeal in a remarkable way.

After her cry for help she rapidly deteriorated and was referred to a clinical psychologist who saw her for an hour a week at the hospital with her mum. In school she was an emotional wreck and was withdrawn and disconnected. Sometimes she wouldn't even communicate with me on a one-to-one basis, and the rest of the class were bewildered and upset around her. With her permission, I began to act as go-between because she hardly spoke to her peer group at all. They wanted to play with her, they wanted to comfort her and, to their credit, they never gave up on her. We worked out an acceptable system of fielding questions and I attempted to tell them how Karen was feeling when they asked. I had no idea what she was really thinking but I could check out with her if she was sad, worried, tired or frightened, etc. and convey this to her friends. I tried sometimes to give reasons so they could make sense of things such as: 'Karen's crying because she thinks she'll get her maths wrong' and 'She's a bit too sad today to play this playtime but she wants to watch you'. I was always touched by their readiness to come up with statements of support: 'I could sit and do her maths with her' or 'I don't mind watching with her'. I believe that they came to realise that she was just that much more extreme than they were – perhaps not a million miles away from them on a bad day. She would sob silently, skulk on the edges of the classroom, panic over very small difficulties, tear up her work, destroy her own belongings, glower at people and refuse to speak. I have to admit that I often felt irritated with her 'lack of progress' because all this time she was coming to school and doing very little except listening. At a more reasonable level, however, I knew there would be no 'quick fix' for this traumatised little girl and that I could not give up on her. I had to stay with it.

Six months into her journey with the clinical psychologist Karen brought some of her work into the classroom and demanded that I take a more active part in her learning. One lunch hour, while the children were in class eating their packed lunches, I was clearing up my things to go to the staff room. She had refused to get her lunch box and was rocking herself in the corner amidst the noise and bustle. I looked across and gave her a reassuring smile and she reached out her hand to me. Her disclosure was humbling and she risked all to share it with me. It was a huge step forward for her. She described what it had been like waiting in that carnage, believing that the car crash was her fault. She thought she should have done more for the people who were injured. It was her job and her fault. All this she had carried these last months. After she had talked about it she asked for a hug and sobbed silently for a good five minutes. Then, in a way that only a child can do, she decided to have her lunch and then go out to play!

With her permission I shared this with her mother and the psychologist. Things were on the way up from then on and she gained strategies to cope with her memories and her feelings.

In the later stages of her journey a girl called Stephanie befriended Karen. One day she asked me:

'Why does Karen panic when we learn something new?'

'Well, you could ask her why.'

'Yes, but I want to know what you think.'

'Well, maybe it's because she doesn't always feel good about herself. Then she thinks she'll get everything wrong.'

'Yes, I think so too. When I couldn't say how I felt about my dog I couldn't do anything. I was horrible then wasn't I?'

'Steph, you're absolutely right. Can you believe you did all those things then! You're so different now aren't you?'

'No. I'm still me.'

The broad beam of her smile said it all. I think I understood a bit better that it is not the core child who changes but her behaviour. With behaviour suddenly deteriorating, as in Karen's case, I could see attitudes towards her changing as quickly, bringing with them further difficulties for her to cope with. How easy it is to get into a downward spiral and to lose sight of the child herself. Karen's temporary difficulties became part of the shared history of our class and enabled other children to develop awareness and initiative. I could not have supported her for so long without the body of the class sharing some part of Karen's struggle. Together we fashioned ways of being compassionate and sticking with the day-to-day difficulties. It was not appropriate that we delved into her private world or got involved in the details; the clinical psychologist and the family were there for that. Nevertheless, the brunt of her distress came with her to school every day and effectively blocked her academic learning. Her emotional growth and learning were huge, however, and she made it back towards independence with the support of this extended team.

Final thoughts

This chapter has been about working to support individual children in such a way as to take their needs into account but without highlighting their deficits or increasing their EBD label. The tension is obvious. We are proposing an individualised 'best fit' that includes rather than isolates. Where a child is outside the expectations of the rest of the class we seek to support them from where they are, trying to move them forward. This may involve steadily bringing the child back to the same expectations we hold for the rest of the class. To do this we use the idea of elastic boundaries which pull the isolated child towards the group whilst the group itself shifts and recognises the difficulties of the individual and moves to meet his or her needs. To do this, we have seen the importance of a teacher's positive attitudes and of his/her ability to reflect systemically; the importance of support from a range of other people including parents and colleagues; of involving the child in his/her own education; and of a willingness to stay with the difficulties until the child can 'lose' his/her label and become an ordinary member of the class. For some this final stage may not be possible but a change on the part of the individual and a greater acceptance on the part of the group is always possible.

Bibliography

Aspy, D.N. and Roebuck, F.N. (1977) *Kids Don't Learn from People They Don't Like*. Amherst, MA, Human Resource Development Press.

Bennett, N. (1987) 'Children Do It In Groups – or Do They?', in J. Thacker (ed.), *Working in Groups, Educational and Child Psychology*, 4(3/4). Leicester, British Psychological Society.

Bowlby, J. (1946) *Forty-four Juvenile Thieves: Their Characters and Home Lives*. London, Balliere, Tindall and Cox.

Buhler, J. and Aspy, D. (1975) 'The Relationship between Physical Fitness of a Selected Sample of Student Teachers and their Performance on the Flanders Verbal Interaction Scale', in J. Buhler and F. Roebuck (eds), *Physical Health for Educators: A Book of Readings*. Denton, TX., North Texas State University Press.

Burland, R. (1978) 'The Evolution of a Token Economy in a School for Maladjusted Junior Boys', *Journal of the Association of Workers with Maladjusted Children*, 7: 65–79.

Burn, M. (1964) *Mr Lyward's Answer*. London, Hamish Hamilton.

Burns, R.B. (1982) *Self-Concept Development and Education*. London, Holt, Rinehart and Winston.

Burt, C. and Howard, M. (1974) 'The Nature and Causes of Maladjustment among Children of School Age', in P. Williams (ed.), *Behaviour Problems in School*. London, University of London Press.

Button, L. (1974) *Developmental Group Work with Adolescents*. London, Hodder and Stoughton.

Cooper, P. (1999a) 'Changing Perceptions of Emotional and Behavioural Difficulties: Maladjustment, EBD and Beyond', *Emotional and Behavioural Difficulties*, 4(1) (Spring): 3–12.

Cooper, P. (ed.) (1999b) *Understanding and Supporting Children with Emotional and Behavioural Difficulties*. London, Jessica Kingsley Publishers.

Cooper, P., Smith, C. and Upton, G. (1994). *Emotional and Behavioural Difficulties*. London, Routledge.

Coopersmith, S. (1967) *The Antecedents of Self- Esteem*. San Francisco, W.H. Freeman.

Croll, P. and Moses, D. (1985) *One in Five: The Assessment and Incidence of Special Educational Needs*. London, Routledge and Kegan Paul.

Cronk, K. (1987) *Teacher–Pupil Conflict in Secondary Schools*. Lewes, Falmer Press.

Department of Education and Science (1975) *The Discovery of Children Requiring Special Education and the Assessment of their Needs: Circular 2/75*. London, Department of Education and Science.

Department of Education and Science (1978) *Special Educational Needs* (Warnock Report). London, HMSO.

Department of Education and Science (1989) *Discipline in Schools* (Elton Report). London, HMSO.

Dowling, E. and Osborne, E. (eds) (1994, 2nd edn) *The Family and the School: A Joint Systems Approach to Problems with Chidren*. London, Routledge.

D'Zurilla, T. and Goldfried, M. (1971) 'Problem-Solving and Behaviour Modification', *Journal of Abnormal Psychology*, 78: 107–26.

Feest, G. (1992) *Listening Skills*. Crediton, Southgate.

Galloway, D. and Goodwin, C. (1987) *The Education of Disturbing Children*. London, Longman.

Gergen, K. (1985) 'The Social Constructionist Movement in Modern Psychology', *American Psychologist*, 40: 266–75.

Gordon, T. (1974) *Teacher Effectiveness Training*. New York, Peter H. Wyden.

Hall, E. and Hall, C. (1988) *Human Relations in Education*. London, Routledge.

Hall, E., Hall, C. and Leech, A. (1990) *Scripted Fantasy in the Classroom*. London, Routledge.

Hargreaves, D. (1967) *Social Relationships in a Secondary School*. London, Routledge.

Hargreaves, D. (1982) *The Challenge of the Comprehensive School*. London, Routledge and Kegan Paul.

Heron, J. (1996) *Cooperative Inquiry*. London, Sage.

HMSO (1992) *Marriage and Divorce Statistics*. London, HMSO.

Hopson, B. and Scally, M. (1981) *Lifeskills Teaching*. London, McGraw-Hill.

Jobling, M. (1976) *The Abused Child: An Annotated Bibliography*. London, National Children's Bureau.

Johnston, C., Patenaude, R. and Inman, G.A. (1992) 'Attributions for Hyperactive and Aggressive Child Behaviours', *Social Cognition*, 10: 255–70.

Kelly, G. (1955) *The Psychology of Personal Constructs*. New York, Norton.

Kitsuse, J. (1962) 'Societal Reactions to Deviant Behaviour: Problems of Theory and Method', *Social Problems*, 9: 247–56.

Lennhoff, F. (1960) *Exceptional Children*. London, Allen and Unwin.

Lodge, C. and Watkins. C. (1999) *Targeting Strategies – Hit and Miss*. Coventry, National Association for Pastoral Care in Education.

McNamara, S. and Moreton, G. (1995) *Changing Behaviour*. London, David Fulton.

Miller, A. (1996) *Pupil Behaviour and Teacher Culture*. London, Cassell.

Ministry of Education (1945) *The Handicapped Pupils and School Health Service Regulations (S.R. and O No. 1076)*. London, HMSO.

Moustakas, C. (1959) *Psychotherapy with Children*. New York, Ballantine Books.

Nias, J. (1989) *Primary Teachers Talking*. London, Routledge.

Ofsted (1999) *Principles into Practice: Effective Education for Pupils with Emotional and Behavioural Difficulties*. Office of Her Majesty's Chief Inspector of Schools.

Plowden, B. H. (1967) *Children and their Primary Schools*. London, HMSO.

Power, M.M., Alderson, R., Phillipson, C.H., Schoenberg, E. and Morris, J.M. (1967) 'Delinquent Schools?', *New Society*, 10: 542–3.

Ravenette, T. (1972) 'Maladjustment: Clinical Concept or Administrative Convenience?', *Journal of the Association of Educational Psychologists*, 3(2): 41–7.

Reynolds, D. and Sullivan, D. (1981) 'The Effects of Schools: A Radical Faith Restated', in B. Gillham (ed.), *Problem Behaviour in the Secondary School*. London, Croom Helm.

Richards, I. (1999) 'Inclusive Schools for Pupils with Emotional and Behavioural Difficulties', *Support for Learning*, 14(3): 99–103.

Roe, M. (1965) *Survey into Progress of Maladjusted Children*. London, Inner London Education Authority.

Rogers, C. (1983) *Freedom to Learn for the '80's*. London, Merrill.

Rosenthal, R. and Jacobson, L. (1968) *Pygmalian in the Classroom*. New York, Holt, Rinehart and Winston.

Rutter, M. (1972) *Maternal Deprivation Reassessed*. Harmondsworth, Penguin.

Rutter, M. (1976) 'Sociocultural influences', in M. Rutter and L. Hersov (eds), *Child Psychiatry: Modern Approaches*. Oxford, Blackwell Scientific.

Rutter, M. and Madge, N. (1976) *Cycles of Disadvantage*. London, Heinemann.

Rutter, M., Maughan, B., Mortimore, P. and Ouston, J. (1979) *Fifteen Thousand Hours: Secondary Schools and their Effects on Children*. London, Open Books.

Shaw, O. (1965) *Maladjusted Boys*. London, Allen and Unwin.

Speed, B. (1991) 'Reality Exists O.K.? An Argument against Constructivism and Social Constructivism', *Journal of Family Therapy*, 13(4): 395–409.
Spender, D. (1982) *Invisible Women: The Schooling Scandal*. London, Women's Press.
Stacey, M. (ed.) (1970) *Hospitals, Children and their Families: The Report of a Pilot Study*. London, Routledge.
Szasz, T. (1972) *The Myth of Mental Illness*. St Albans, Paladin.
Thacker, J. (1983) *Steps to Success: A Course in Problem-Solving, 11–13*. Slough, NFER-Nelson.
Thacker, J. (1990) 'Working through Groups in the Classroom', in J. Jones and N. Frederickson (eds), *Refocusing Educational Psychology*. London, Falmer Press.
Thacker, J. (1994) 'Organizational Cultures: How to Identify and Understand Them', *Educational and Child Psychology*, 11(3): 11–20.
Thacker, J (1998) *Using Cooperative Inquiry to Raise Awareness of the Leadership and Organizational Culture in an English Primary School*. Lampeter, The Edwin Mellen Press.
Thacker, J. and Feest, G. (1991) 'Groupwork in the Primary School', in G. Lindsay and A. Miller (eds), *Psychological Services for Primary Schools*. London, Longman.
Thomas, A. and Chess, S. (1977) *Temperament and Development*. New York, Brunner Mazel.
Tuckman, B.W. (1965) 'Developmental Sequence in Small Groups', *Psychological Bulletin*, 63: 384–99.
Tuckman, B.W. and Jensen, M.A.C. (1977) 'Stages of Small Group Development Revised', *Group and Organization Studies*, 1: 419–27.
Wahl, W. (1999) 'Helping Children with Emotional and Behavioural Difficulties', *Self and Society*, 27(1): 21–4.
Watkins, C. and Thacker, V.J. (1993) *Tutoring: INSET Workshops for a Whole School Approach*. London, Longman.
Watzlawick, P., Weakland, J. and Fisch, R. (1974) *Change: Principles of Problem Formation and Resolution*. New York, Norton.
Wheldall, K., Bevan, K. and Shortall, K. (1986) 'A Touch of Reinforcement: The Effects of Contingent Teacher Touch on the Classroom Behaviour of Young Children', *Educational Review*, 38(3): 207–16.
Willis, P. (1977) *Learning to Labour*. London, Saxon House.
Wills, D. (1960) *Throw Away Thy Rod*. London, Victor Gollancz Ltd.

Index